THE DEVELOPMENT OF
LANGUAGE AND LITERACY

MARIAN WHITEHEAD

SERIES EDITOR TINA BRUCE

Hodder & Stoughton

A MEMBER OF THE HODDER HEADLINE GROUP

Orders: please contact Bookpoint Ltd, 78 Milton Park, Abingdon, Oxon OX14 4TD.
Telephone: (44) 01235 827720, Fax: (44) 01235 400454. Lines are open from 9.00 - 6.00, Monday to Saturday,
with a 24 hour message answering service. Email address: orders@bookpoint.co.uk

British Library Cataloguing in Publication Data
A catalogue record for this title is available from The British Library

ISBN 0 340 64414 1

First published 1996
Impression number   10 9 8 7 6 5 4 3
Year   2005 2004 2003 2002 2001 2000 1999

Typeset by Wearset, Boldon, Tyne and Wear.
Printed in Great Britain for Hodder & Stoughton Educational, a division of Hodder Headline Plc,
338 Euston Road, London NW1 3BH by Scotprint Ltd, Musselburgh, Scotland.

This book is dedicated to my family who cherish me and make everything worthwhile – 'I'm practising wearing purple'!

Acknowledgements

My thanks to the following students, teachers, schools, families and children who generously shared their photographs and materials with me: the nursery and reception teachers at Myatt Garden Primary School, Lewisham, for allowing me to quote from their observations; Allyson Pascoe and Comet Nursery School, Hackney, for figure 4 and the photographs in Chapter 4; Judith Crampton and Lucas Vale Primary School, Deptford, for the photographs and book reviews in Chapter 5; Ellen Sizer and Louise for the 'lecture notes'; Davina Grant for the nursery messages; Gill Wilson and Athelney Primary School, Catford, for Martha the pig; and Sue Hirschheimer and Tunstall Nursery School, Croydon, for figure 32.

Special thanks to my family for photographs and materials and for continuing to educate me. Thanks also to my early childhood research colleagues at Goldsmiths' College for their affection and support – I needed it!

Contents

Series Preface – 0–8 Years

At most times in history and in most parts of the world, the first eight years of life have been seen as the first phase of living. Ideally, during this period, children learn who they are; about those who are significant to them; and how their world is. They learn to take part, and how to contribute creatively, imaginatively, sensitively and reflectively.

Children learn through and with the people they love and the people who care for them. They learn through being physically active, through real, direct experiences, and through learning how to make and use symbolic systems, such as play, language and representation. Whether children are at home, in nursery schools, classes, family centres, day nurseries, or playgroups, workplace nurseries, primary schools or whatever, they need informed adults who can help them. The series will help those who work with young children, in whatever capacity, to be as informed as possible about this first phase of living.

From the age of eight years all the developing and learning can be consolidated, hopefully in ways which build on what has gone before.

In this series, different books emphasise different aspects of the first phase of living. *Getting to Know You* and *Learning to be Strong* give high status to adults (parents and early-childhood specialists of all kinds) who love and work with children. *Getting to Know You*, by Lynne Bartholomew and Tina Bruce, focuses on the importance of adults in the lives of children. Observing children in spontaneous situations at Redford House Nursery (a workplace nursery) and in a variety of other settings, the book emulates the spirit of Susan Isaacs. This means using theory to interpret observations and recording the progress of children as they are supported and extended in their development and learning. The book is full of examples of good practice in record-keeping. Unless we know and understand our children, unless we act effectively on what we know, we cannot help them very much.

Learning to be Strong, by Margy Whalley, helps us to see how important it is that all the adults living or working with children act as a team. This is undoubtedly one of the most important kinds of partnership that human beings ever make. When adults come together and use their energy in an orchestrated way on behalf of the child, then quality and excellent progress are seen. Pen Green Centre for Under-fives and Families is the story of the development of a kind of partnership which Margaret McMillan would have admired. Beacons of excellence continue to shine and illuminate practice through the ages, transcending the passing of time.

Just as the first two books emphasise the importance of the adult helping the child, the next two focus *on* the child. John Matthews helps us to focus on one of the ways in which children learn to use symbolic systems. In *Helping Children to Draw and Paint in Early Childhood*, he looks at how children keep hold of the experiences they have through the process of representation. Children's drawings and paintings are looked at in a way which goes beyond the superficial, and helps us to understand details. This means the adult can help the child better. Doing this is a complex process, but the book suggests ways which are easy to understand and is full of real examples.

In *Helping Children to Learn through a Movement Perspective*, Mollie Davies, an internationally respected movement expert with years of practical experience of working with young children, writes about the central place of movement within the learning process. In a lively, well-illustrated book, with lots of real examples, she makes a case for movement as a common denominator of the total development of children, and in this draws our attention to its integrating function. In addition to linking movement with physical development and movement with thinking she helps us to see how children's expressive and social behaviour can also be looked at through 'movement eyes'. She suggests ways in which its role can be highlighted in a variety of learning and teaching settings with a whole chapter devoted to dance – the art form of movement. The provision of a readily accessible movement framework gives excellent opportunities for adults to plan, observe and record their children's development in movement terms.

Self-Esteem and Successful Early Learning by Rosemary Roberts is about the importance of being positive, encouraging and gently firm in bringing up and working with young children. Whilst every family is different, every family shares some aspects of living with young children. These are taken up and given focus in the book in ways that are accessible and lead to practical strategies. The reader meets a variety of situations with the family and explores successful ways of tackling them so that the theories supporting the practice become meaningful and useful.

The Development of Language and Literacy by Marian Whitehead emphasises the importance of the people children meet, and the need for adults to be sensitive to the child's culture, feelings and developing ideas as conversations are made, and early attempts to communicate in writing and reading emerge. Children need to spend time with people who care about them, enjoy being with them, and support their language.

Clinging to dogma, 'I believe children need . . .' or saying 'What was good enough for me . . .' is not good enough. Children deserve better than that. The pursuit of excellence means being informed. This series will help adults to increase their knowledge and understanding of the 'first phase of living', and to act in the light of this for the good of children.

TINA BRUCE

INTRODUCTION

This book is about the most exciting and important aspect of human development – language in the early years. It is a book for parents, carers, teachers and other workers, because they work and play with very young children and share in the emergence of their language. I hope it will support early years carers and practitioners by giving them a confident understanding of children's language development in the years from nought to eight.

This is undoubtedly rather challenging, but no more so than the daily demands of caring for and educating young children in a variety of settings. The approach I have taken tries to avoid too many artificial divisions and watertight categories such as those which set apart academic language studies from guidelines for practice, or from our daily talking, thinking and coping. Or those which carefully parcel out children's activities as pre-school or school, reading or writing, or 'only scribbling' and 'only talking'. My approach is not watertight – it is very leaky (this is known as holistic in academic jargon) and attempts to work with the rich mixture of thinking, feeling, imagining, talking, listening, drawing, writing and reading which is typical of all our language activities. In order to do this I shall draw on the knowledge and wealth of child observations to be found in many academic studies. I shall also draw on my own experiences of watching and listening to very young children, while being a teacher, a mother, a granny, a researcher and an eavesdropper in the supermarket check-out queue.

This holistic approach is responsible for the range of topics covered in the book. It begins with an account of how language first develops and then moves on to explore the achievements and challenges of young bilinguals. The discussion of the significance of stories, narrative and playing with language builds a kind of bridge from understanding spoken language to the topic of literacy. Literacy is tackled in two chapters, one with a pre-statutory school emphasis and one with a focus on the years from five, and even four, to eight – the years of statutory schooling in the UK. This division should help to keep the discussion of such a complex topic manageable, but it also reflects the reality of schooling arrangements in the UK. This divide poses an important challenge for parents, teachers and early years workers to ensure continuity of good language learning for children from nought to eight. The book ends with some suggestions for making the all-important partnership with parents a focus for talking about children's language development.

Language, the early years and National Curriculum English

I referred above to the UK compulsory schooling divide which has for decades split the traditional and international definition of the early years as covering either age three to eight, or even birth to eight. Since 1988 the National Curriculum for England and Wales has deepened and formalised this divide by introducing legally binding requirements setting down the precise curriculum content to be taught in the first Key Stage to children from the age of five to seven. In reality many four-year-olds are in reception classes and experience the National Curriculum and the inevitable pressures caused by the tests which mark the end of each Key Stage. Meanwhile, eight-year-olds in England and Wales are now at the start of Key Stage 2 and increasingly likely to become the forgotten early years children as older primary approaches absorb them. The situation in Scotland is far less tightly structured because the 5 to 14 Guidelines are exactly as their name suggests – guidelines for professionals to adapt and interpret.

The recent restructuring of schooling in Britain has its own political and administrative logic, but this has little to do with the patterns of child development. This is particularly true of the development of language which is studied from the moment of birth as a continuous process, and is arguably at its most exciting in the first three to four years of life. Serious students of language find all forms and varieties of language exciting and informative and few are comfortable with the notion that 'English', as opposed to 'language', is at the centre of the curriculum.

English is one of the three core subjects of the National Curriculum and consists of three attainment targets: speaking and listening; reading; writing. The general requirements for English are summarised in the DFE's Orders for 1995:

> *English should develop pupils' abilities to communicate effectively in speech and writing and to listen with understanding. It should also enable them to be enthusiastic, responsive and knowledgeable readers.*

Recent 'Nursery Education' proposals for the guidance of providers and for the inspection of institutions with under-fives focus on 'desirable outcomes' in six areas of learning, including language and literacy (SCAA, 1996).

This book will be exploring all these important topics, but under the label of language development and in an appropriately leaky or holistic way!

Glossary

This is a brief collection of some of the terms which are used by linguists in order to discuss languages clearly and accurately. It will help you if language study is new to you and it also indicates the range of topics to be found in this book.

Bilingual

Referring to varying degrees of fluency in two languages; often including literacy as well as spoken language. Bilingual can refer to an individual or a community.

Monolingual
Fluency and/or literacy in one language and applicable to an individual or a community.

Multilingual
Referring to degrees of fluency and/or literacy in several languages; can refer to an individual or a community.

Cognition

This refers to the ability to think and can include understanding, representation, perception, reasoning, memory, etc. It is of great significance for language study because thought and language are closely linked.

Grammar

The rules governing human language or individual languages; also the study of such rules.

Phonetics
The study of the speech sounds made by the physical vocal system.

Phonics
A method for teaching reading which trains beginners to recognise the sound values of letters.

Phonology
The study of the organisation and patterning of sounds in languages.

Semantics
The study of meaning in language.

Syntax
The organisation of words into meaningfully ordered combinations; also small changes made to words to indicate, for example, plurals and past tenses.

Linguistics

The study or science of language.

Linguist
One who studies linguistics; can also mean one who is competent in several languages.

Metalingual
The language used for talking and writing about language; or, language about language.

Psycholinguistics
The study of language as a major expression of human thinking and learning: literally, the shared area of psychology and linguistics.

Sociolinguistics
The study of language in use in all possible social contexts: literally, the shared area of sociology and linguistics.

Literacy

The ability to read and write a language, or languages.

Genre
A distinctive form of writing, like a poem or a travel guide.

Representation

An important form of thinking which uses actions, pictures, objects or words to stand for ideas and experiences. Quite literally we 're-present' something in order to think about it: a child's drawing of a cat, or saying 'miaow', are representations.

Sign
Closely related to symbols (see below) and representation, a sign is usually far more specific and part of a system of conventions: for example, a red traffic light

or any of the combined hand and facial signs used in signing systems for the deaf.

Symbol

Essentially something which stands for a total experience or sequence of ideas. Symbols may be as diverse as national costumes, a handshake or a proffered drink. They are derived from representational thinking. The particular marks used in a writing system are sometimes called symbols.

Variety

In linguistics this refers to the huge number of human languages which exist, as well as to the variations found in any apparently single language community. These varieties within a language include accent and dialect. **All speakers have accents and use one or more dialects**.

Accent

This refers to matters of pronunciation: the sound qualities of the language as it is spoken by individuals and groups. There are geographical-regional, social class and educational variations in accents.

Dialect

A dialect is a variety of a language and includes distinctive vocabulary and syntax systems. Dialects were originally rooted in specific geographical regions, but historical and cultural events have made some dialects more prestigious and some more despised than others.

Register

This refers to the repertoire of appropriate styles which we all use for differing social settings. We change our ways of speaking and writing according to the who, where, when and how; these changes of register reflect differing degrees of formality.

Standard English

This dialect is the standard or 'norm' for communicating in English in the public, educational, professional and commercial spheres. It is not a regional variety but it has great prestige because it is 'the norm'. There are, however, a number of different forms of Standard English in Britain and worldwide.

1 THE DEVELOPMENT OF LANGUAGE

The story of language development is a saga which has its share of unsolved mysteries and discoveries and, like all good stories, it helps us to understand more about being human. 'A miracle' or 'a mystery' are words often used about the development of language, mainly because linguists cannot account in full for the speed and the apparent ease with which almost all babies acquire the essential structure of one or more languages in their first three years. When I first wrote an account of early language acquisition (Whitehead, 1990a) I called it 'The Big Questions' in order to draw attention to the important questions which this special kind of linguistic study, called psycholinguistics, asks. Two big questions occur again and again: how do we learn to understand and use our first languages, and what are the links between language and thinking? This last question often surprises interested folk who just want to know how we all learn to speak and use words, although a moment's thought will show that words and conversations are all about communicating and sharing meanings. So, the study of early language development involves both language study, or linguistics, and the study of mental processes and learning, or psychology. These two aspects of human behaviour – language and thinking – account for much of what makes us both unique individuals and sociable persons firmly tied to our families and cultural groups. Indeed, I would argue that in learning more about language development we are finding out about human nature. You will have to judge whether I have exaggerated here, but this book will try to explain how we become talkers, thinkers and mark-makers.

THE PUSH-PULL LANGUAGE GAME

For centuries people have been fascinated by the mysteries of language and some bizarre ideas inspired the earliest alleged linguistic experiments. Caring for a group of babies in strict silence and hoping that their first words would be in Latin is one legendary example. Cutting out and eating the tongues of defeated Roman soldiers in the hope of acquiring Latin is another! Legend has it that the babies died and no results from the tongues experiment are available to researchers (Mills and Mills, 1993, p. 6). More recent research and speculation is less colourful and a lot kinder, but it is just as fascinated by the commonplace yet stunning nature of acquiring language. Furthermore, modern scientific approaches are still trying to sort out 'the babies' and 'the tongues' theories about the development of early language. Does language burst out fully formed from infants, or do they have to learn it all from the speech communities they are born into?

Modern approaches are increasingly likely to point out the truth in both these extremes and suggest what I would describe as a push-pull theory. (This 'push-pull' is a metaphor and not to be confused with the actual push and pull movements of children's early mark-making described by Matthews, 1994a.) The infant is pushed into language by her own powerful inner drive to communicate and share meanings, while, simultaneously, relationships with her carers who use specific languages pull her into a shared world of language. While it is clear that language will not develop if adults never speak to babies, it is also clear that babies have their own communication skills and some innate ability to process the language around them.

The broad patterns in this complicated process will be outlined in the following sections, but early years carers and educators should be proud that the research is based on those traditions of careful child-watching and listening familiar to us all. The history of such approaches is outlined in an earlier volume in this series, along with detailed guidance on getting to know young children and keeping a variety of records (Bartholomew and Bruce, 1993). Linguists, families and other professionals have used notes, sketches, diaries and the more recent audio and video technologies to build up records of events such as infants' eye-gaze, expressions, smiles, mouth noises, recognisable and repeated sounds, gestures, first words and early conversations. An example of a mother's language diary of her child's first words (figure 1) shows that detail and accuracy are far more useful than polished presentation.

COMMUNICATING WITHOUT WORDS

Spoken recognisable words are not at the start of language and communication. A child's first word has behind it a personal history of listening, observing and experimenting with sounds and highly selective imitations of people. Similarly, the art of conversation is rooted, well before talk, in the innate sociability and sensitivity of infants. It has been known for many years that newborn babies are most attentive to human voices, faces and eyes. They will spend surprisingly lengthy periods of time just gazing into the eyes of their carers (Schaffer, 1977; Stern, 1977). Adults on the receiving end of this adoration invariably respond by gazing back, smiling, nodding and talking to the baby 'as if' they were conversing with an understanding partner. They frequently stroke the baby's face, chin and lips, perhaps to emphasise the physical sources of human speech.

DATE	AGE	WORD	MEANS	COMMENTS 1,03 = book
6.12.87	0,10	'boo'	book	1,02 just for books; applies to books, newspapers, pictures
23.12.87	0,10	'bā-bā'	bye bye	accompanies waving
24.12.87	0,10	'a-(l)-o'	hallo	1,02 general + also for telephone; into toy telephone receiver
29.12.87	0,11	'gō'	gone	4/88 → gone; when had/drink finished
1.1.88	0,11	'ma-ma'	Mummy	5/88 → Mummy
1.1.88	0,11	'da-da'	Daddy	5/88 → Daddy
8.1.88	0,11	'bā'	bath	
17.1.88	0-11	'pooh'	...	5/88 → pooh poohs
30.1.88	1,00	a-pa	apple	(hum hum – yum yum)
~~28.1.88~~	~~1,00~~	cuckoo	~~Knock~~ Sienna + for 'boo' ~~Knock~~	
7.2.88	1,00	'up'		lifting up; also for down + change of position
26.2.88 appr	1,00	'dó' → no NO		→ 4/88 'no' (1,02 to open
28.2.88	1,01	'gā'	cat	5/88 → 'cat'
8.3.88	1,01	'de da'	'Goda'	flower – and you → now you are
13.3.88	1,01	'es'	yes	
13.3.88	1,01	gā	car	
13.3.88	1,01	Dada gone		
15.3.88	1,01	do-do	doggy	(toy one) + real
16.3.88	1,01	'cane'	...	
18.3.88	1,01	'uck'	sock(s)	? → ock
18.3.88	1,01	'keys'		
20.3.88	1,01	'choo'	shoe(s)	
21.3.88	1,01	'boo'	...	used in conjunction with 'cuckoo'
22.3.88	1,01	'at'	hat	1,02 also for 'hair'
22.3.88	1,01	'ock'	walk	
23.3.88	1,01	bo'	ball	4/88 → ball
23.3.88	1,01	'pus'		
23.3.88 appr	1,01	'ot'	hot	
23.3.88	1,01	Ka-Ka	cracker	
23.3.88 appr	1,01	'otoo'	out	5/88 → 'out'; want to go outside.
27.3.88	1,02	bush	brush	
27.3.88	1,02	dollo	dolly	
28.3.88	1,02	op	soap	
28.3.88	1,02	door		

Figure 1 *A mother's language diary of her child's first words*

Even at a few weeks old the infant's love affair with people is shown by different reactions to persons, as opposed to interesting objects. Moving objects may be watched and reached for, but people, especially a carer, are responded to with smiles, lip movements and arm waving (Trevarthen, 1975, cited in Harris, 1992). Getting into relationships with people probably begins in the earliest hours of life: many newborns will imitate adult face and hand movements (Trevarthen, 1993). The list of actions imitated is interesting: for example, mouth-opening, tongue-poking, eye-blinking, eyebrow movements, sad and angry expressions, and hand opening and closing. Bearing in mind that all these actions are used in normal speech production and conversations, it is clear that this early non-verbal kind of communication is the foundation for communicating with words all through our lives.

There is widespread agreement among researchers that by five or six weeks babies and their carers are regularly involved in mutually satisfying conversational activities. Infants frequently take the lead and set the pace and carers respond, even to the extent of imitating their babies. So what is significant about this for early language learning? It would appear to be something to do with the complex business of getting two minds in contact (Trevarthen, 1993), because the exchange of meanings and language are at the centre of human communication. Although the first things shared may only be eye-contacts, smiles and sounds, these quickly lead on to other possibilities. Infants and carers start to follow each other's line of gaze, or attentional focus, and then it is but a short step to pointing, special noises, and word-like sounds. Traditional games with babies like peek-a-boo, dropping and recovering objects or giving and taking food and toys, have their own special words which are repeated again and again in highly predictable ways. Just saying or making noises, gestures and facial expressions to indicate 'please', 'thank you', 'boo' and 'bye bye' are the ordinary and unremarkable basis for getting in touch with another mind. It is done by the playful use of actions, noises and objects which stand for ideas and feelings.

First words

What is a word? This is a question which students of early language development, including many parents and carers, often ask. The answer will have to start with sounds, for sound is the very stuff of language, but any old sound produced at random will not be a word. Most linguists would expect a word to have the following additional characteristics:

- it is produced and used spontaneously by the child;

- it is identified by the caregiver who is the authority on what the child says (Nelson, 1973);

- it occurs more than once in the same context or activity (Harris, 1992).

The sound-making, or phonological, skills of infants are immature and go through many changes, so word identification is not easy and it is important to have this rather elaborate way of clarifying what counts as a word. The emphasis on spontaneity is there to exclude simple imitations, because a word should signal the child's first attempts to identify and communicate meanings. We can only be certain this is happening if the child's use of the new word is fairly consistent, or appropriate to the context in which it is uttered. This is where the agreement of the regular caregiver is so important; only the child's partner in the games and non-verbal conversations described above knows enough about the contexts in which first words occur.

   Many studies of first words are undertaken by the parents of young infants (Engel and Whitehead, 1993) and the intimate insights of professional linguist-parents have shown how some words begin to emerge as early as nine months (Halliday, 1975). At this stage the words are sounds which are personal to the infant, used consistently for requesting and indicating interest, and quite recognisable. We might want to think of these as embryo-words, noticed mainly by professional linguists, but there is no mistaking the breakthrough into 'real' words when it occurs. Many parents and carers can recall years later the first words spoken by their children, but it is important to bear in mind that the onset and the rate of acquisition of early words is highly variable and personal. Most babies do begin to say their first words somewhere between 12 and 18 months, but there can be earlier starts, as well as much later ones. The real value of records of children's first words is not the totals and the scores, but the windows they give us into children's minds and their views of their families and the world.

   My granddaughter's first word was 'book', produced at ten months and sounding much like 'boo'. An outsider would have been ignorant of the richness of experience behind that single syllable word. In fact, like many of the first words of young infants, it stood for a whole sentence. It was a 'come-and-read-to-me-now' word and referred to a daily ritual which involved clambering on the couch with a pile of picture books; snuggling up to the chosen adult; then sharing in pointing at and naming pictures, and listening to rhymes and stories (figure 2). All this wealth of experience, organisation and meaning was carried by one word, hence the great importance of a carer's knowledge about the

Figure 2   'Book' meant 'come-and-read-to-me-now'

context of first words. Carers can also alert us to the fact that first words develop and change, because my granddaughter was soon using 'book' to include all the magazines and newspapers which came into the house.

First words can only be fully understood within the contexts in which they are uttered, but they do indicate how the young child is noticing and sorting out the world. Collections of first words are usually about such things as family members, daily routines, food, vehicles, toys and pets. These groupings are known to linguists as semantic fields because they reveal the sets of meanings around which a child's first interests and language development are clustering. And it is not surprising that people, food, animals and possessions are highly interesting to babies and need labels early on! These semantic sets also include those important words which get people to do things for you, such as 'up', 'walk', 'out' and 'gone'. The field of meaning here is part of the lifetime study of human relationships and people management. Two other very important words are acquired in these early days – 'no' and 'yes' – and usually in that order. At this point the young talker has joined the language club (Smith, 1988) and is well on the way to learning about self-assertion, as well as cooperation.

More words

Single words can pack a linguistic punch, but they do have their limitations. They depend a lot on context and on the interpretive sensitivity of a carer. However, their power and flexibility increases greatly when they are combined together in order to say more complicated things. Infants vary greatly in the rate, the frequency and the complexity of their early word combinations. My grandson was a very creative word combiner, starting with 'door uppy' (open the door) at 20 months and progressing to little stories by 22 months, such as 'sea Daddy park it car' (Daddy is parking the car by the sea). The striking thing about these utterances is that they are unique to the child, their originality is a reminder that they could not have been copied from carers or the language community. They use quite different word order: in the first example the important object of attention, the door, is named before the desired action is indicated. A similar reversal happens in the much longer example and again suggests that the focus of the child's attention is named before the rest of the action is described. This is a very useful strategy for gaining a listener's attention. In the latter incident the small boy was very impressed when the car was driven right on to the beach. It literally was parked by the sea!

These examples help us to see that the beginning speaker is creative, determined and resourceful as he or she struggles to use a limited hold on speech in order to communicate important new meanings. My grandson's limitations were partly physical in terms of making a range of sounds in his mouth and throat and controlling air-flow and muscles; his limitations were partly linguistic in terms of the range of vocabulary and conventional grammatical structures he knew; and at not quite two years old he had a limited range of life experiences. Yet it is at this early stage in language development that professional linguists get very excited about what young children are doing when they first start to combine words together.

The reason for all the excitement is grammar. These small children are able, in their second year, to combine words together in original ways which convey meanings to others. This is a standard definition of a grammar (see the next section). Furthermore, they have not been taught the system they have hit upon for doing this and it certainly differs from the conventions of adult language use, but it is systematic, it has a pattern and it works. It communicates meanings to users of the conventional language system. In other words, it is an early emerging grammar. Linguists describe grammars in terms of the things that they enable us to do with language, so what can these little children do with their early language system?

My 16-month-old granddaughter rushes into the bathroom shouting 'dirty hand wash it', and her mother is left in no doubt that she wants help to remove garden soil from her hand. Her newly emerging grammar helps her to use language in order to gain the interest and cooperation of other people – it gets things done. My grandson was heard to say at 20 months, as the family cat left by the kitchen window, 'no more miaow', a lovely comment on the absence of the cat and a skilful recycling of comments like 'no more apple'. Grammatical word combinations of this sort gave him a way of commenting on the world and any particular state of affairs.

So, the emerging language system enables very young children to do two important things: to get things done, including involving other people, and to comment on the world. Similar conclusions about children's earliest meaningful language have been reached by linguists and researchers (Halliday, 1975) and it is interesting to think about how important these two functions of language remain for us all through our lives.

Is this grammar?

If we do not have some understanding of what a grammar is, we are likely to go along with the majority of people who would dismiss the examples above as ungrammatical. Yet I have already claimed that linguists see early word combinations as an important development: the first evidence of grammatical speech. Why then is there considerable disagreement about the nature of grammar? The answer to this and to most other linguistic disputes, of which there are many, is that the modern study of language is constantly battling against deeply held beliefs and prejudices.

Prescriptive grammar

On the one side we have those beliefs about language which emphasise correctness and rules; rules which tell us how we *ought* to speak and write. This is known as prescriptive grammar: it prescribes what we ought to do. These rules hark back to a supposedly 'logical' and 'more grammatical' language, in fact to Latin, and are attempts to squeeze 'vulgar' and 'illogical' languages, like English, into ill-fitting Latin shoes. When this fails, as it must, speakers are instructed to speak like a book, using the rules of written language in their speech. This approach was the dominant view of grammar until the early years of this century and it still has a great hold on the minds of most people. It was the accepted way of teaching English in schools, particularly the grammar and public schools of Britain, until well into the 1950s and the results are sometimes desperately sad.

Why should this be so? Firstly, a prescriptive approach divides the nation into those who think that they can and do speak like the classical rule books of grammar, and those, the majority, who have a strong conviction that they do not even speak their own home language properly. Secondly, it supports a damaging belief in language league tables; some languages just are better, more logical and more sophisticated than others, goes the old argument. This is a particularly dangerous view because of the close identification of groups of people with their language: if the language is judged to be primitive or inadequate, so are its users. Thirdly, so many of us are convinced that grammar is difficult, boring and irrelevant to our lives that you may have already decided not to read this section of the book. Finally, it leads to a serious undervaluing of young children's stunning achievements in learning their languages in the first few years of life.

Descriptive grammars

On the other side, however, is modern linguistics which has much to say about the human mind, about learning and about grammar – but not a lot about Latin! The three main dimensions of modern views of grammar are highly relevant and interesting to parents, carers, teachers and other human beings.

Firstly, modern grammars are descriptive. This means that they are not rigid rules about how we ought to speak and write – they are attempts to describe how we actually do so. There are complex sets of rules which govern the ways in which the sounds of a language, or its written symbols, are linked to meanings and messages. In attempting to describe these, modern linguists behave like any other scientists: they observe, listen, keep records and make informed guesses about what is going on. And they can disagree and even be proved wrong. That is why I frequently write 'grammars' as a plural; there are several in circulation, but I shall only refer to what they have in common.

A second distinguishing feature of modern grammars is that they are described as having three, or possibly four, levels. These are phonology, syntax, semantics and lexis.

Lexis

Lexis is the optional extra which can be added to the big three and it may be more familiar to you as 'vocabulary'. The lexis is all the stock of words available to a speech community and those words appearing in the dictionaries of a written language.

Phonology

Phonology is the organisation and patterning of the sounds of a language, including such important elements as emphasis and intonation. These give different languages their distinctive 'tunes', the rise and fall of questions and statements, as well as the stress we put on important words, or parts of words. Phonology also records the regional and social variations of sounds among speakers of the same language. These pronunciation differences are commonly known as *accents*. The study of phonology also includes an understanding of the physical processes involved in making the sounds we call language.

Syntax

Syntax is concerned with words and the ways in which they can be modified and changed themselves, as well as combined together in groups. This is the one aspect of a modern grammar which is a close family relative of the prescriptive grammar referred to above. However, there is a crucial difference: modern syntax records and analyses what is heard and written in a living language community. The rules of syntax emphasise those word changes and word orders which affect meaning and communication. In English 's' added to a noun usually means more than one and many verbs indicate where an action was in the past, or is completed, by adding 'ed'. Word order is also an interesting carrier of meaning: 'woman bites dog' gets a different reaction from 'dog bites woman', even if you are not a news-hungry journalist! In the same language community there can still be differences between distinctive groups of speakers in the vocabulary and the patterns of syntax they use; this affects word order, the ways of showing tenses (time), number (singular or plural) and possession. These varieties within a language are called *dialects*; their origins are regional and social and among the most frequently discussed in the UK are the several varieties of standard English (see Glossary).

Semantics

Semantics is the study of meaning in a language and takes us well beyond the surface of words, sounds and questions about 'who bit whom', and into the workings of the mind. There are also historical and cultural dimensions to the study of semantics. Word meanings change over time and have dramatically different effects on our perceptions. Only specialist scholars appreciate the real impact of Shakespeare's use of words such as 'presently' and 'weed', but we all know that in that same period 'mistress' carried a range of meanings different from its twentieth-century use. Different cultures categorise and label the world differently: the colour spectrum, pets, possessions and food are all classified in such diverse ways that a dog can be for dinner, a mat for praying, and a book a sacred object.

The third characteristic of a modern grammar takes us into the next section of this chapter, because a grammar is now taken to be a description of some aspects of the human mind. The rules of grammar do not come from Latin, they originate in the mind.

LANGUAGE AND THINKING

The fact that modern linguists are finding out more about how we learn anything when they study small babies learning their languages is an important reason for asking the carers and educators of under-eights to take some interest in linguistics. The claims made this century about language, the mind and thinking are all based on lengthy, in-depth studies of babies and young children and have increased our knowledge of psychology, language and culture. Among these claims is the notion that some kind of universal grammar is pre-programmed in our minds (Chomsky, 1957), so that all human languages have some underlying similarities. This would account for the ease and speed with which babies all over the world learn to use and understand languages, rapidly becoming skilled linguists and communicators.

Other approaches have looked at the ways in which the early language used by a child in communicating with his or her carers turns inward to change and enrich the ways in which the child can think (Vygotsky, 1986; Bruner and Haste, 1987). A further outcome of this is that language enables us to think in a symbolic way. That is, words can begin to stand for objects and people, even when they are not around: 'I want my mummy' cries the small child left with another carer. Or we can name feelings and experiences which cannot easily be pointed to in the world: fear or loyalty, for example. Whole categories of experience are summed up and expressed symbolically by children who have begun to use words, but the complexity of learning words and labels is frequently underestimated (Aitchison, 1994).

A rich symbolic system such as that provided by language is necessary if children are to communicate and share in the life of a culture. This is very important, particularly if young children have the kind of serious sensory damage associated with deafness and blindness. The systems of signing and touching used by the deaf and the blind enable them to classify and order their feelings and experiences, make original observations about their world and gain the social cooperation of others (Sacks, 1989). Although we must not underestimate the language and learning problems encountered by blind or deaf children, it is known that they have, like unimpaired children, their own personal and variable patterns of development. Interestingly, the development of syntax in these children is normal, although the early stages of vocabulary acquisition are slightly delayed (Harris, 1992). This indicates, yet again, that there must be an inner pre-programmed language ability in all children which has its own momentum. It is the social and cultural aspects of learning a particular language, for example by playing 'naming' games with a carer ('what's that'; 'where's your nose'), and acquiring vocabulary, which will show some initial delay.

LATER DEVELOPMENTS

It is quite usual for books and articles about language development to be mainly concerned with the first three or four years of life. This is not due to a lack of interest in the later years of early childhood, but a reflection of the linguistic facts. By the age of six the major features of adult speech and language are all in place, although this is not to say that other developments and enrichment do not occur. Literacy is one such development, but it must piggy-back on the achievements of the earliest months and years outlined in this chapter.

I have doubts about the existence of easily identifiable ages and stages in language development, but the following rough guide may help to complete the map of what comes after longer combinations of words.

From two to four

This is the golden age of grammar when little children show that they have a mind for rules, even if their community language is apparently inconsistent. For the English-speaking child this involves attempts to tidy up irregular plurals and add 's' to all of them, resulting in 'mouses' and 'foots'. It also shows up in the totally spontaneous and un-imitated regularising of irregular past tenses, so that little children claim to have 'goed' to the shops and 'rided' on the bus. These errors are ones to cheer about, for they are evidence that the child's mind is a powerful tool for processing and producing the rules of language. A similar piece of evidence that the language-creating mind of the child is working well at this stage is the occasional turning of nouns into verbs. This tendency already exists in many languages: we use a brush 'to brush' our teeth and a rake 'to rake' the leaves. Some three- and four-year-olds have been heard to talk about 'lawning' (mowing the lawn) and announce 'I seat belted myself' (Clark, 1982, pp. 390–402).

During this period children's longer word combinations become easier for adults to understand because they are linked together, as sequences of cause and effect, by the gradual trial-and-error use of 'and', 'because', 'if' and so on. Children's questions no longer rely solely on a rising tone of voice, but use the linguistic terms 'why', 'who', 'where' and 'how'.

If this is the golden age for grammar, it is also the great leap forward in vocabulary, with something in excess of 1600 words in the average four-year-old's spoken vocabulary and vastly greater numbers of words understood (Crystal, 1987). Many young children also begin to enrich their word store with words and linguistic structures which are not from everyday life, but from oral poetry and storytelling, and from the world of books. My grandson was overheard singing his own half-remembered versions of nursery rhymes at 21 months: 'diddle, diddle . . . John . . . on shoes'. His sister was telling herself the story of *Meg and Mog* (Nicoll and Pienkowski), from the book, at the age of two years: 'it's a lady . . . looking at in the mirror . . . it's a mirror . . . a jumper . . . there's a coat? . . . she has to go out? . . . this is the way to go? . . .'

By the age of four the physical maturity of the nervous system and the finer muscle control over the mouth, throat and tongue, and even the presence of teeth, make the young child's pronunciation of languages very much closer to the adult forms and easier to understand.

From five to eight and beyond

In the later years of early childhood children's language developments are increasingly influenced by their wider social experiences and the impact of literacy. There is still some fine-tuning of the system to take place, but it is probable that even this depends on social experience and the influence of literacy. Children may begin to use tentative language such as 'perhaps' and 'probably' but this reflects talk, schooling and book language, as does the ability to handle negative forms like 'scarcely' and 'hardly'. There is some evidence of a late-developing grammatical feature known as the passive voice, when the usual word order of 'who does what to whom' is reversed and we learn that 'the dog was bitten by the woman'. Children's understanding of who was biting whom in this news item is often confused until the later primary years – it is a very literary form.

In these later years we have to trace the pattern of language development in children's ever-increasing exposure and reactions to other people, other children, other languages, written language and the literacy tools of their culture: namely, pictures, television, films, books, stories, poetry and, of course, schools.

Last words

Certain conclusions may be drawn from this tour of language development.

- Children are sensitive and sociable communicators from birth.

- Children's language is original and creative and enables them to get things done, gain the cooperation of others, and comment on their world.

- Language is one of the major developments of infancy and, alongside play and other ways of representing experience like dancing, singing and painting, shapes thinking, learning and literacy.

- Speaking and listening must be at the heart of all our provision for care and education in the years from nought to eight.

- Conversations with interested adults are essential to children's linguistic, emotional, social and cognitive welfare.

- Early years carers and educators can learn more about their children by observing them and listening to them. In order to do this we can keep brief notebooks, word diaries, audio and video records, and photographs.

It follows that all early years settings must be organised around talk and play between children and adults, and between children and children.

2 Young Bilinguals

The previous chapter contains many examples of early language collected from my own grandchildren – examples which are probably very similar to those heard in most English-speaking households and pre-school care and education settings. At this point I would like to complete the picture of these two children learning to speak by filling in the details of the social, cultural and family setting which provided the backdrop for their language development.

Firstly, although the children were born into a home where English was the main language of communication with them in their earliest months and years, their parents and paternal grandparents (who shared the home) were also fluent communicators in German, Hebrew and Hungarian (see Engel and Whitehead, 1993). Secondly, the children were involved in songs, rhymes and playful dancing and bouncing routines which used traditional German, Hungarian and Hebrew language forms. Thirdly, the household was in Israel and the Hebrew language also came into the home through friends, relatives, neighbours, radio, television and, in the written form, through newspapers, advertising and many other kinds of printed materials. Fourthly, the children's expanding world of shopping, visits, playing with other children and attendance at Hebrew-speaking kindergarten made the older child a fluent bilingual by the age of four.

Finally, it is important to emphasise the significance of the attitudes to bilingualism in the wider society in which the children lived. Both their main languages are highly valued: English has a quasi-official status because of the history of Israel. Furthermore, bilingualism is considered normal and to be expected in a society of immigrants and settlers.

In many young children's lives complexity and diversity in their languages, cultures and relationships are not uncommon.

Young bilinguals – who are they?

Young bilinguals are like the children described above, in that their language and family situations are complex and uniquely varied. Furthermore, it is very common for several languages and different kinds of writing systems to be involved in so-called bilingualism. This is why it is important to start from real examples of the kind I have given before going on to define what is involved in being bilingual. Otherwise we can fall into the trap of inventing a totally straightforward, but unrealistic 'picture of a bilingual'. A picture which seriously undervalues the achievements and skills of young bilinguals.

A very strict definition of the term 'bilingual' is 'speaking two languages' and, although this applies with a degree of accuracy to many children and adults, the strict definition does not reflect the variety of family and cultural language experiences described at the beginning of this chapter. When individuals and families use more than two languages we should describe them as 'multilingual', a term I prefer myself. However, the convention of using the term bilingual for all children able to use two or more languages is widely accepted in the field of child care and education and I shall use it here. We also need to be aware that the focus of this chapter is on the individual child's experience of bilingualism, but it is essential to remind British readers of the existence of whole societies, and groups within societies, who are bilingual: for example, the citizens of Belgium, Switzerland and Quebec, and speakers of Catalan and Welsh. This is known as *societal bilingualism* (Baker, 1993), but it also plays a significant part in the individual bilingual's development and attitude towards the maintenance of her or his languages. Thus the speed and ease with which my grandchildren became bilingual are not unrelated to the linguistic situation in Israel which is officially bilingual (Hebrew and Arabic) and, in practice, multilingual.

Recent trends in defining individual bilingualism are moving away from the idealised notion of someone who is perfectly fluent in two languages: usually called a *balanced bilingual*. Definitions now try to reflect the complexity of life with two or more languages and highlight such things as:

- degrees of changing competence in speaking several languages;

- the different situations which prompt the use of one language rather than another;

- the range of literacy skills in different languages;

- the effects of changes of country of residence, and other upheavals, on an individual's bilingualism.

Changing competence

Changing competence acknowledges the infant who adds the first two words of her second language to her rapidly expanding first language vocabulary at 14 months (Whitehead, 1990b): she is an emerging bilingual. It also defines my own holiday attempts to shop for a few basics and politely pass the time of day in Greek as a kind of bilingual performance. It is possible for individuals to be anywhere on a bilingual continuum, from fluency and literacy in several languages to limited understanding, or very 'rusty' spoken competence, in one other language.

Different situations

The notion of different situations focuses on the linguistic choices made by fluent young bilinguals who may be quite happy to use one language with English granny, another two languages with Israeli granny, and yet another language with friends in kindergarten. This 'language switching' is a common occurrence among fluent bilinguals and occurs at the levels of words, phrases and sentences and in all kinds of combinations. The reasons for it are said to include group loyalty, politeness, excluding strangers, emphasis, clarification, and even simple tiredness. There is no evidence, however, that it is due to linguistic incompetence and confusion. Very young emerging bilinguals often do 'language mixing' which involves combining words from several languages in their simple utterances. This may reflect an early stage of learning to separate their different languages (Arnberg, 1987), but it is not a symptom of muddle and inadequacy. Indeed, many researchers would agree that young bilinguals associate particular people with particular languages in a systematic way, offering instant translations and reassurances to confused monolingual carers! Some of these very young emerging bilinguals also choose, or mix in, words from any of their languages which can be most easily pronounced.

Literacy skills

A range of literacy skills is now acknowledged in any definition of bilingualism, as is an appreciation that young children may already be aware of the variety of writing systems being used in their families and communities. It is quite common to be a speaker of a language and not a writer of it. Some people read a language they do not speak, and some languages do not have a written form. There are also languages which use a highly prestigious form for official or sacred writing and a different form for everyday communication.

Thus many young children may be familiar with writing systems which are written horizontally from right to left, not just from left to right, and others may see a script which moves vertically down the page from top to bottom. There are also many children in British early years settings who speak a regional dialect such as Sylheti in their homes (figure 3), are beginning to read and write Bengali in community schools, and are also learning to read Arabic in order to study the Koran.

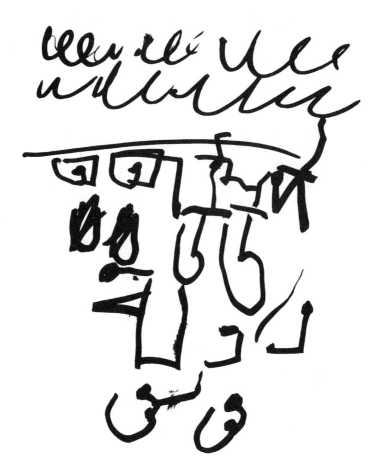

Figure 3   A four-year-old Sylheti-speaking child in a London reception class has written a shopping list in the home corner

Effects of changed circumstances

The effects of changed circumstances on any individual bilingual's languages can be so varied that it is impossible to generalise, but we can note a few significant influences. For example, the death or departure from the household of an important adult speaker may remove the source of one language. Relocation from one kind of language community to another will have significant effects: cultural attitudes to bilingualism may be different and the lack of any need for one particular language may result in an apparent loss of that language. In *Generations of Memories*: *Voices of Jewish Women* (Copperman *et al.*, 1989) Ena Abrahams writes about the sadness of losing the language which she spoke in childhood. In this case the language, Yiddish, was not then respected and its use often led to ridicule and discrimination. A more optimistic picture is painted by some linguists who note that rarely used, but valued, family languages can remain 'dormant' until successfully re-activated by a return to the appropriate language community (Saunders, 1988).

LEARNING FROM YOUNG BILINGUALS

Young bilinguals have important lessons to teach us about language and about learning. They can also enrich our understanding of the diversity of human culture and challenge our prejudices about languages and people. The following lessons from young bilinguals are grouped under the headings of *language*, *thinking* and *culture*, but there is plenty of leakage between the categories and our deepest feelings about our languages affect all of them.

Language

- All human languages are, as Chapter 1 indicated, equally complex. They are patterned by rules and able to meet all of the needs of their speakers.

- Bilingualism, including multilingualism, is the natural way of life for millions of people around the world and even in the UK over 100 languages are in routine use, not including the native British Celtic languages (Crystal, 1987).

- The pattern of individual language development is broadly similar in monolingual and bilingual situations: it is a combination of the infant's unique experiences with a general sequence of stages (see Chapter 1). At first words and word combinations come from all of the languages in use and the separating out of their distinctive grammars occurs later.

- A general language ability underlies all human language competence, but the bilingual has more than one particular linguistic and cultural way of expressing and using this universal ability.

- When bilinguals are acquiring other languages they may use a strategy of 'bridge building' to get from a known language to a new language. This often involves using words from the new language, but with the grammatical patterns of the securely known language. This is a skilled temporary solution called 'interlanguage' by linguists (Selinker, 1992).

Many of the apparent linguistic 'mistakes' made by young bilingual learners are highly successful strategies for language learning.

Thinking

- The mind is not a container with a limited capacity for language. There is no truth in the belief that the use of more than one language necessarily reduces the individual's ability in each language.

- Following on from this, we must be clear that bilingualism is not a handicap, particularly not an educational handicap. Nor is it an exotic peculiarity which turns bilingual speakers of any age into oddities and targets for ridicule (Mills and Mills, 1993).

- These common misunderstandings and prejudices about languages and thinking lead to bad policies at national and local levels. Carers and educators may even feel obliged to suppress or downgrade children's bilingualism and impose 'English only' as soon as possible.

- Bilingualism has many advantages, not least being the young linguist's marked ability to get 'outside' a language in some way and see it as just one of several options for labelling and categorising the world. Young bilinguals are able to explore the sounds and the meanings of several languages, as well as the differing ways of representing them in writing (Gregory and Kelly, 1992).

Young bilinguals have the potential ability to think about the system behind languages and this can give them an early advantage in literacy learning.

Culture

- Long before words come, young bilinguals learn the body language and the tunes of their linguistic community. They also start to understand the complex interplay of personal relationships and attitudes in bilingual households. This means that young bilinguals soon become remarkably sensitive to social situations and can make subtle judgements about such things as appropriateness, power, self-expression, formality, dialects and the whole business of linguistic choices.

- Young bilinguals start like all babies; they use movements and vocalisations to get them into the language communities of their immediate carers. Talk is the crucial factor in the social and intellectual development of any child, whether bilingual or monolingual. Talk asserts the identity and self-esteem of the young speaker: it says 'Here I come, look at me!' Talk builds relationships with others, gets things done, makes sense of the world and becomes a crucially important tool for thinking, whatever the language used.

- Languages tether all of us to particular places, people, communities, stories and myths. Young bilinguals who share in the tales, rhymes, jokes, songs and gossip of their varied language groups have access to a remarkably rich range of human cultural experiences. Professional carers and educators need to believe that the bilingual situation is potentially life-enhancing.

Young bilinguals do not see their languages as a problem, they simply are a fact of life: the only life these children know. It is monolinguals who must sort out their own confusions and understand that the bilingual is an integrated person, not the sum of two monolinguals (Hamers and Blanc, 1989, p. 257).

HELPING YOUNG BILINGUALS

This section can only skim the surface of an important subject and it is influenced by the following publications which I recommend for further reading:

Foundations of Bilingual Education and Bilingualism, Colin Baker (1993; 1996);

Bilingualism in the Primary School, Richard W. Mills and Jean Mills (1993);

Teaching Talking and Learning in Key Stage One, NCC/National Oracy Project (1990).

These books are mainly focused on children as they move through compulsory schooling, but the following principles apply to much younger children speaking first languages other than English, as well as to any form of early years setting.

Respect

It is absolutely essential that early years carers and educators respect the languages of the young children for whom they are responsible. This must go deeper than vague goodwill or tolerance. It means that we have to create environments in which children find their languages and cultures welcomed and reflected in photographs, signs, pictures, fabrics, equipment and play materials. However, the labelling of doors and toilets will not send the right messages about respect for 'other' languages if these languages are never used in the high status areas of books, language and numeracy. Parents from all communities want their children to be confident and successful in traditional 'academic' areas, but there is evidence that professional educators and carers across Europe know little about the rich and diverse community literacy backgrounds of young bilinguals (Spencer and Dombey, 1994). We should continue to share the festivals, foods and songs of our children's diverse cultures, but we should also work harder at knowing more about their languages. We should know how to name them correctly – Israeli and Pakistani are not languages, for example – we could learn to count in them, as well as using the essential greetings and the 'please' and 'thank you' forms which oil the wheels of social life.

Curriculum

A curriculum is not just the subjects taught in schools. It is all the learning opportunities we provide for children; all the behaviours we encourage, or discourage; as well as all the routines we set up in group settings and the ways in which adults regularly interact with children (EYCG, 1992). A clear rationale for this notion of curriculum in the early years is provided by Bartholomew and Bruce (1993, pp. 22–3) in this series. The important point to be made here is that any curriculum content or activity which is good for young bilinguals is good for all young children. This is because an acceptable early years curriculum for bilinguals extends their thinking, self-esteem, language, literacy, creativity, problem-solving, social skills and understanding of the world. What more could we want for young monolinguals?

Early years settings

Early years settings are potentially the most appropriate learning contexts for young bilinguals who are engaging with English for the first time. This is because these settings have had well-established traditions of active learning through play, exploration, investigation and all the accompanying talk. Doing real things that matter, in the company of interested adults and with other children, and talking about what occurs, is just like the settings in which we all learn our first languages. Good early years settings can be very like home language settings because they provide what linguists call 'genuine contexts' (Mills and Mills, 1993). In other words, food is bought, cooked, sniffed, tasted, talked about and shared for eating, because that is what people do with food and it really matters; not because it teaches money and fractions, or the solubility of salt! Genuine contexts are even more powerful language learning situations if a monolingual adult in charge needs to be told how to cook and eat unfamiliar foods. The adult becomes a vulnerable learner, the bilingual child becomes a knowledgeable teacher, and the linguistic and communicative strategies of both are at full stretch.

An enormous amount of natural linguistic repetition and imitation goes on in richly resourced informal early years settings, *if* children are able to choose from a range of materials, activities and flexible social groupings, and have access to several caring and interested adults. Think of the constantly repeated language forms you use about people, materials, equipment, places, routines and actions in your own professional setting. Add to this all the shared language between children which adults only catch a hint of, and the potential for children to imitate and rehearse new language forms unobtrusively will strike you. Linked to this issue of trying out a new language safely and without going public in the early stages, is the need for a relaxed and unpressured setting in which 'time to stand and stare' and take it all in is allowed. We all become speakers of a first language after a lengthy period of just listening, watching, doing things, trying a few rough approximations and getting really enthusiastic feedback. It is important that early years settings provide a safe place for just watching, listening and joining in, and avoid any emphasis on premature and meaningless verbalising. But children's spontaneous communications and tentative attempts to find the right words should be warmly received and respectfully modelled back to them.

Professional strategies

The single most powerful strategy we can adopt in order to support and extend the education and care of young bilinguals is to upgrade the *oral* nature of the curriculum in all early years settings.

Talk in early years settings has been discussed above, but the special quality of oral communication, the 'way' of saying things, is crucial when we are attempting to share meanings. This requires a much greater use of informative body language, eye-contact, facial expression, gesture and mime.

We also need to think about how we use our voices in multilingual situations and learn to cultivate a clear professional style of expression and pronunciation. It is helpful to vary the speed, pitch and volume of speech, according to the circumstances, so that young non-English speakers are helped to develop an ear for the sound patterns of natural spoken English. They are not helped by being shouted at, given military-style orders, spoken to in a non-English reminiscent of 'Janet and John', or addressed in adult baby-talk.

It is helpful if we can increase the amount of repetition and rephrasing we use in our speech so that children hear alternative ways of formulating the same ideas and messages. This makes for what linguists call rich input and helps the listener to get a grip on meanings and expressions. Of course all these strategies are dependent on genuine contexts and real situations for talk, as discussed earlier.

Stories, rhymes and songs must be at the heart of a good oral curriculum which supports and extends young bilinguals and monolinguals. This kind of material is highly motivating: children and adults alike are spellbound by the human interest in a well-told or well-read tale, and are caught up as a group in the rhythms of poetic language and music. The linguistic power of story, rhyme and song stems from the predictability of 'what comes next' in such material. Gaps in the story or rhyme can be anticipated by the most inexperienced listener or 'other language' speaker who soon manages a 'huff' and a 'puff' or a well-placed 'quack'!

Perfect examples of incidental language lessons are found in both traditional and modern stories: bilinguals can join in the frequent repetition of phrases such as *Not Now Bernard* (McKee), *Bye Bye Baby* (Ahlberg), *We're Going on a Bear Hunt* (Rosen) and *Oi! Get Off Our Train* (Burningham).

The provision of taped versions of favourite rhymes, songs, stories and poems increases the amount of exposure young learners get to poetic and bookish English. These tapes may be commercially produced, but a large number can be made by carers, teachers, adults who work with the children, members of the local community and even older children. This material gives young children a taste for independent learning: they can choose to listen to and practise well-loved chunks of the language over and over again. Other kinds of 'story props' will be discussed in a later chapter, but it is worth emphasising at this point that they are crucial to the developing bilingualism of young learners.

Areas of the curriculum in an early years setting which enhance oral language development and bilingualism include provision for imaginative role play and drama; music making of all kinds; drawing, mark-making, writing and painting; play with a range of malleable materials such as clay and dough; play with natural materials like water and sand; block-play and constructing models with junk and scrap materials; gardening and investigating out-of-doors areas; making and using puppets of all kinds; sorting, grouping, sharing and counting everything; and buying, preparing and cooking food.

I appear to have outlined an early years curriculum in its entirety, or the whole of human life! But that is the secret of success in early bilingual provision. Young bilinguals do not need limited input and restricted environments. They must have things to do, materials to comment on, people to interact with, exciting experiences to organise and talk about, and richly varied models of a new language to work on.

The potential richness of the early years curriculum can be the key to success for the young emerging bilingual; this suggests two important implications:

- a rich and developmentally appropriate early years curriculum should be retained for all children under eight, including those in the statutory phase of schooling (five to eight);

- all attempts to withdraw children who speak first languages other than English from the main group, or class, should be resisted on linguistic, social and educational grounds.

First language support teaching

This is an issue which rouses many prejudices and also challenges our commitment as a society to truly positive bilingualism, as opposed to assimilation to an all-English-speaking culture as fast as possible. Fear of strangeness, fear of 'foreigners' and desperate competition for good homes, jobs and schools are all expressed as fear of foreign languages. This applies to some languages more than others: French is romantic and Italian is beautiful, but the languages of historically exploited and under-privileged people, or of very remote societies, are despised. Of course it is the speakers, not the language, who suffer when this occurs, although we may fool ourselves into believing that some languages are just not as sophisticated as others. We play the same dangerous game of deluding ourselves about people and language when we dismiss some of the dialects and accents of English as not good enough for education and success in later life.

Early years professionals must always be aware of their own irrational fears and prejudices when they hear some languages, accents or dialects. Very young children should not be at a serious disadvantage from the moment they enter a group setting or open their mouths.

There is evidence that young children who are forced to leave their first languages outside the playgroup, nursery or school will be slowed down as they struggle to acquire new skills and ideas through the medium of a barely understood language. Equally disturbing will be the harm done to the continued development of their home language, or languages, which may become despised and partly discarded. This lack of respect for, and commitment to, first language support in schools and early years settings can lead to the desperate situation for some children of not being linguistically at home anywhere in the world and unable to use any language adequately for thinking and learning.

These issues press particularly hard on early years teachers in the compulsory stages of schooling and there is little reason to be optimistic that the lessons of modern linguistics have been learnt by our legislators. However, we are professionals and must do our best for all children; we cannot sit about and wait for better things to happen. We can use all our ingenuity to create early years settings and classrooms which do not require children 'to cast off the language and culture of the home' as they cross the threshold (DES, 1975). None of us has the linguistic skills to meet the language needs and strengths of all the young emerging bilinguals we work with, but we can recruit language tutors in some unexpected places.

Children as language tutors

We can encourage children who speak the same languages to play together, share activities and talk through the new and the familiar experiences we plan for them in their own tongues.

We can use bilingual children as interpreters and translators for ourselves, for other children and for their families, because the need to explain to others can enhance language skills and self-esteem. But this should be done sensitively and with respect to all the adults and children involved. If badly handled, child interpreting can sometimes expose interpreter, recipient and language to ridicule.

There are some advantages in occasionally 'twinning' older bilingual children with monolingual partners so that they can be supportive of each other in a range of skills and activities, not just language. After all, speaking English is no guarantee of being good at mathematics or climbing.

Young bilinguals can be teachers and enrich early years settings by sharing their songs, rhymes, legends and dances, as well as many other aspects of their lives, with caring and interested adults and other children. One positive effect of this will be to improve the tolerance and sensitivity to diversity in the setting, thus ensuring that a worthwhile moral education is offered to children and early years professionals alike.

Community language tutors

Members of the community are a rich resource and should be welcomed into all early years settings and classrooms, especially if they are speakers of languages used by some of the children.

Many researchers have produced lists of what parents and local community members could help with in schools and other group settings (Mills and Mills, 1993; Houlton, 1986). They do bear repeating as many professionals and institutions have not fully explored the possibilities of working with families and groups of other language speakers.

Remember that they can help by using community languages for:

- telling stories;

- recording stories on audio and video tapes;

- helping children write messages and stories;

- writing stories and reminiscences;

- making books with computers, binders and laminators;

- recording rhymes and songs on tape;

- teaching rhymes, songs, dances and games;

- preparing traditional food and writing recipes;

- teaching counting;

- writing down numbers and counting systems;

- counting with children and making number games;

- playing in the areas inside and outside, including home corners, sand and water provision, construction toys, malleable materials, drawing and painting;

- translating labels, signs, notices, letters, and some books made by English-speaking adults and children;

- writing first language versions of favourite books, stories and poems used in the setting.

Professional carers and educators can, with the assistance of community helpers and families, take the children out into the local area and learn about shops, centres, places of worship and different literacy traditions. These expeditions strengthen the children's sense of place and self-esteem. They also teach carers and educators, if they are prepared to learn, something of a community's ways of teaching its children and its expectations and hopes for them as they experience early years provision.

All early years practitioners can support young emerging bilinguals by valuing the individual child, by valuing talk and by valuing human diversity.

3 Stories, Narrative And Play With Language

The previous chapters have been concerned with spoken language development in early childhood and this chapter will focus on the links between oral language and emerging literacy. The child's growing understanding of these links will not be fostered by ever-earlier formal reading and writing lessons, but by participating in the creation and exchange of stories and playfully exploring the nature of language. The discussion which follows tries to build a bridge from spoken language to literacy, a bridge which takes us from the study of stories and narrative, by way of play with language, to choosing and using literature in early years settings.

Stories

Wherever there are people there are stories. Stories were drawn on cave walls by prehistoric human groups and stories have continued to be sculpted, danced, acted, sung and recited. But most commonly stories are told, so commonly in fact, that we may take them for granted and not appreciate their significance. Yet at all stages in our lives we create and share stories, whatever the occasion.

Stories are basically about the 'what' of human experience and thinking: what I believe, what happens to me, what I know, what I feel. Indeed, any enquiry, whether it be a major research survey (Whitehead, 1994), or just asking after someone's health, is likely to elicit a story. Similar stories, or fragments of stories, created by young children appear frequently in the observations recorded by early years practitioners:

> I sorted out some more paint – some of the jars were empty so I mixed up some more with the children – lots of conversation –
> A: 'Is it hot?' (because the powder paint when poured gave out clouds of dust).

A's question is an analogy drawn from the scientific story she must have been told, probably at home, when she noticed that the process of heating water and food created steam.

A reception class in the same school had listened to an information story about black bears and built a model of a black bear habitat. Their teacher had also provided models of bears for the habitat and observed the children's play with these resources. It is clear that the 'facts' about black bears were remembered and understood by the children because of their experiences of story extended by imaginative play:

> C (five years): Yum, flowers.
> J (five years) No, they don't eat flowers.
> They're very good climbers and swimmers and jumpers, 'cause they're black bears.

Published research is another rich source of early years stories in which the young tellers are apparently pinning down what they know about people, moral values and society:

> Lisa: (Pouring [pretend] tea.) My daddy says black people come from Africa.
> Wally: I come from Chicago.
> Lisa: White people are born in America.
> Wally: I'm black and I was born in Chicago.
> (Paley, 1981, p. 47)

Even at the end of our lives we are still telling stories about what has happened to us, or our families, as many age reminiscence projects have demonstrated:

> Well, my mother saw Queen Victoria when she was a child . . . Anyway, she went in this crowd and my grandfather put her on his shoulders, 'cos she couldn't see very much, and she said: 'All I saw was a very grumpy old lady sitting in a carriage.' She was quite disgusted about the whole thing.
> (Jones and Medlicott, 1989, p. 23)

So what is going on here? What are they all doing, these children and adults from diverse cultures? The short answer must be that they are making sense of their experiences. Not only of things which happen to them, but also of things which they have encountered in the stories of other people. The stories seem to be hooks on which they can hang a significant event, incident or feeling, and hold on to it and revisit it. We do go over our stories again and again; this is very noticeable in gossip, reminiscences, jokes and folk tales. This would suggest that repeating and re-assembling the events of a story is a significant way of thinking about things and sorting them out. So stories are about understanding, a view supported by observations of young children playing. They frequently re-enact and retell stories about puzzling and alarming incidents, as the following observation from a nursery teacher shows:

> *R (Four years ten months) had a nasty cut to the head while outside and had to be taken from the nursery to the hospital. The children were all concerned, there was a lot of blood on the floor. Two members of staff were involved in administering first aid and R was carried to the ambulance. One child asked if R was dead.*
> *A (Four years three months) was particularly disturbed by the accident and clung to his parents after school . . . The next afternoon A constructed himself a white bandeau out of three pieces of paper and wore it round his head. When asked about what he had made he simply replied, 'R's bandage of course'.*

Play is not the only medium through which children rework a challenging story; they frequently use drawing, painting and the manipulation of materials and objects as ways of representing their thinking about experiences. John Matthews explores children's use of drawing and painting in depth, including this aspect of story representation, in an earlier book in this series (Matthews, 1994a). Whatever the medium, the representation is often accompanied by a verbalised story commentary:

> *I'll have to put you in the yard soon – with the horses and chickens and cows. Special department for you – you'll be the only goat. Oh no you won't – 'cos I bought the whole family – I think.*
> (Britton, 1992, p. 74)

In this brief excerpt from a much longer sequence, Clare, at four years eight months, uses a story-like commentary to organise her own drawing and also to manage, with some humour, the boisterous interruptions from her two-and-a-half year old sister who is 'acting the goat'.

At this point we can put down a marker for later literacy: **very young children are soon at ease with story forms and use orally the language structures and ways of thinking about experience which occur in the written system**.

It is also clear that in stories children and adults have a very special tool for thinking about what they encounter. We now need to know more about how this tool works.

NARRATIVE

We have seen that stories fasten on the 'what' of experiences and events, real and imaginary. Narrative, however, is the spoken, written or visual representation that relates a story's events. Narrative is the 'how' of story and is always focused on a telling of some kind. It is an ancient and basic language activity. 'Someone telling someone else that something happened' (Smith, 1980, 1981, p. 228) is at the root of all legends, histories, folk tales, biographies and novels.

Yet narrative is not just random 'telling', it is concerned with time: it sequences events in time in order to tell about them. In this respect it appears to be closely linked with the organisation and functioning of memory. We have already seen, above, how memories are recalled and told as if they were a story.

Narrative is not simply limited to endless lists of events to be told about in temporal order. In fact, we would soon tire of 'and then . . . and then . . .' in any account; it is as if we require something more 'meaty' in our narratives. The meat we look for is some hint of the narrator's attitudes, judgements and values, even if we disagree strongly with them. Narrative is concerned with values and choices and most typically speculates on the human condition, whether the narrative is found in high culture, casual gossip or children's play.

Narrative is the backbone of all the stories we hear and tell. Narrative is a telling which selects and orders events in time and speculates on life and human behaviour. This selecting, ordering and evaluating gives meaning and a pattern to the random sensations and happenings of daily existence.

The evidence to support such a strong claim is found in the narratives created by whole communities, as well as by individuals, and the development of narrative competence can be studied in young children.

Narrative and communities

The explanatory narratives of communities and cultural groups are more familiar to us as myths, legends, folk tales, rhymes, sayings, beliefs and proverbs. These originated in the pre-literate oral traditions of societies, although we now meet most of them fixed in print. They were constantly modified and changed as they travelled down the centuries by word of mouth. Oral narratives held the shared history of a group and constantly reminded both tellers and listeners of enemies, battles, defeats, victories and family loyalties. They were also the holders of a group's beliefs about human origins, values and moral behaviour as well as handy little rules of thumb about anything, from child-rearing to weather forecasts:

spare the rod and spoil the child

red sky at night, shepherd's delight
red sky in the morning, shepherd's warning.

The antiquity of such material can tend to obscure the undoubted fact that cultures and groups still go on making sense of shared experiences and forging group assumptions. This ongoing account lists group successes and disasters and is the central feature of any culture. The dynamic struggle to shape the stories and, therefore, the meanings of a culture, is found in contemporary media, politics and popular entertainment. As societies become more complex and pluralist they generate many apparently conflicting stories: 'the American dream, mom and apple pie' cannot be a relevant story for all American citizens. Similarly, an England of cricket on the green and old ladies cycling to church has little or no explanatory power for many British Bengali families in Tower Hamlets, or children in Belfast, or the black Welsh community of Cardiff. These mismatches arise when narrowly specific stories are forced on a complex society, but broader and more universal narratives about human relationships, our links with the wider society and our aspirations for our children do still evolve and bind communities together.

The significance of these community narratives for young children lies in their function as useful ways into the shared beliefs and meaning-making strategies of the culture. We all know 'the big bad wolf' as a kind of shorthand for danger and threat in the wider world. Similarly, Anansi can represent human cunning and ingenuity, while Cinderella is an almost universal symbol of the triumphant maturity of the poorest and most undervalued child. Community narratives are ready-made resources which children shape to their own needs as they parade through playrooms and gardens being 'the queen', 'the police', or 'superman'.

Community narratives help to build the literacy bridge because they are often the first and most familiar written materials introduced to young children, in the form of traditional rhyme and story books, religious texts and folk tales.

Personal narratives

The need to record our own existence and make some mark in the world is at the heart of our personal memories and daydreams, as the stories at the start of the chapter indicated. The community, or cultural group, provides some helpful blueprints (Hughes, 1995) as we have seen, but individual narratives are about personal identity and the pleasures and difficulties of particular relationships.

In recent years researchers and scholars have built a very strong case for the claim that narrative is a primary function of the mind and the organising principle of memory (Hardy, 1977). Our constant storytelling about almost everything is now seen as a kind of 'brain fiction' (Gregory, 1977) which creates and then mulls over a whole range of possibilities. It is as if we plan lots of possible strategies and scenarios in story form before taking action. This brings us very close to behaving like scientists who always have a possible story-like explanation for any event, only they call their brain fictions hypotheses. We are all, young children and adults alike, creators of imaginary worlds and stories which enable us to try out alternatives, predict possibilities and make sense of experience.

Very young children are often in the same position as the research scientist: they are constantly meeting new events and situations and must create some kind of predictive and explanatory story which will help them to cope successfully. This is shown in their extraordinary skill in making up story-hypotheses about what they observe, whether it be the 'steam' from the powder paints (above), or the problems of age and growth as experienced by Mollie at two years eleven months:

> 'I'm not too big to reach that,' she says, trying to hang up her jacket. 'But my already birthday is going to come now. Then I can be big to reach it.'
> (Paley, 1986, p. 4)

Mollie reminds us that personal narratives create ways of thinking about abstract and difficult ideas and formulating hypotheses which can be modified in the light of further experience and information. These processes are more usually described as learning.

The personal narratives of young children are exciting glimpses of learning as it occurs. They are also acts of self-assertion and identity. Once again these narratives can be linked with early language and mark-making because they assert 'I am here, I exist, look at me'. There is some evidence of a developmental pattern in the growth of children's narrative competence. For example, carers make up little stories about their infants' appearance and personalities, literally from birth, and repeat these tales to their infants again and again. Two-year-olds alone in bed are able to tell themselves the story of their day: not only do they talk about events and interactions with important people, they also try out and practise new words and invent nonsense rhymes (Nelson, 1989). From two years children take over and use the narratives and literary conventions of their immediate culture. Here is Lem, a black two-year-old in the USA, explaining to himself the unexpected sound of a bell:

> *Way*
> *Far*
> *Now*
> *It a church bell*
> *Ringin'*
> *Dey singin'*
> *Ringin'*
> *You hear it?*
> *I hear it*
> *Far*
> *Now.*
> (Heath, 1983, p. 170)

The style and influence of memorable and highly participatory visits to a gospel church are clear in this little song – as clear as the traditional story book language in three-and-a-half-year-old Adam's opening lines:

> *Hey listen to me*
> *I'm going to tell a story*
> *Once upon a time*
> *there were three little crocodiles*
> *named Flopsy, Mopsy and Cottontail . . .*
> (Sheridan, 1979, p. 12)

This narrative continues as a tale of wish-fulfilment and narrowly averted disasters which have more to do with Adam's desires than the adventures of his famous characters. It is clear that Lem and Adam are mulling over their experiences and thinking about 'me' in the world.

Personal narratives are bridges to literacy because they involve young children in thinking and using language like real writers. They formulate story-like hypotheses and scenarios about their lives and experiences and 'tell it like' the oral and literary traditions of their cultures.

The roots of literature

The strong impulse to narrate everything enables children to learn about the world by selecting, ordering, evaluating and predicting. This narrative drive also prepares children for the literary forms of their culture by accustoming them to being in the role of storytellers about their own lives. More than that, they also learn to tell stories about themselves and their families, as if they were characters in books:

> [Wally:] *Once there was a boy hunter. His little sister didn't like him so he ran away. So he found a baby girl lion.*
> (Paley, 1981, p. 29)

Early years professionals are so familiar with this kind of spoken narrative that they may fail to be impressed by it, yet what is happening is at the heart of literature and literacy. Five-year-old Wally is an expert at talking like a book and fictionalising himself and his concerns. He has been supported in this by the traditional stories and rhymes he has heard in kindergarten, and the gossip and narratives he has participated in at home.

Literature reflects our human narrative competence; it selects and orders events in order to tell about them, it makes meaningful patterns out of random occurrences and it speculates on the chances of life. Literature also introduces us to more people and experiences than we can ever encounter in reality in one lifetime; it enriches our lives immeasurably and extends the possible range of our attitudes, values and responses. Literature does all this for very young children, as any adult who has shared *Noisy Nora* (Wells) or *Six Dinner Sid* (Moore) with a young child will know.

Literature is also special in its treatment of language. Such things as selection, pattern and order are very obvious in the language of story and poetry and the effects of sounds, rhymes and repetition are carefully orchestrated. This special language arrests our attention, demands repetition and lodges in the mind. Along with our children we know 'Humpty Dumpty' and 'Hickory Dickory Dock' off by heart. We are also aware that these rhyming mini-narratives have a strange and disturbing playfulness.

PLAY WITH LANGUAGE

Sounds

Linguists have often noted that very young children enjoy playing about with the sound possibilities of the languages they are in the process of learning, even if there is no one around to hear them. The following example from the pre-sleep monologues of two-and-a-half-year-old Anthony explores the alliteration and the rhyming possibilities of English:

bink
let bobo bink
bink ben bink
blue kink
(Weir, 1962, p. 105)

This delightful example comes from a famous study which inspired many later researchers, but the 'father' of this tradition of listening to young children's play with language was Kornei Chukovsky.

Nonsense and reality

Chukovsky's study of Russian two- to five-year-olds was written in the 1920s and demonstrated that children do not simply muck about with the sounds of a language, they also play with ideas and turn reality on its head. The explanation for this 'topsy turvy' play with ideas is that it is a confirmation of children's grasp of reality. Jokes and nonsense depend on knowing the right way to do things. This certainly explains the appeal of nonsense verse and nursery rhymes, as well as the determination with which little children take imaginative liberties with words, objects and information:

> Adult: *'Isn't there something to eat in the cupboard?'*
> Child: *'There's only a small piece of cake, but it's middle-aged.'*
> (Chukovsky, 1963, p. 3)

A more recent British study of the spoken vocabulary of five-year-olds (Raban, 1988) revealed that there was a surprising amount of language used by them which can only be described as poetic, or nonsensical. At the time little was made of the fact that the children were frequently saying such things as 'oops-a-daisy', 'rock-a-bye', 'ding-a-dong' and 'rat-a-tat-tat', although nursery rhymes and games with carers are clearly the source of this material.

Early phonological awareness

It is now increasingly clear, and well documented, that very young children's later success in reading is partly related to their early knowledge of nursery rhymes and their sensitivity to rhyme and poetically repetitive sounds in their languages (Bryant and Bradley, 1985; Goswami and Bryant, 1990). This knowledge is now called early phonological awareness. Regular phonological patterns can be heard in the beginning sounds of words and when these are the same we call them alliteration. Repeated and similar sounding endings are called rhyme. Many poor readers in primary schools are remarkably insensitive to rhymes and to the beginning sounds of words, but very young children with an interest in the sounds and poetry of language may well be on the road to reading, writing and spelling successfully.

IMPLICATIONS FOR LITERACY

We need to be aware of these findings and supportive of young children's interest in language, sounds, nonsense and play with words. This suggests a curriculum rich in many kinds of music, songs, poetry, chants, riddles, tongue-twisters and jokes, as well as all kinds of verbal nonsense, from 'knock, knock' jokes and 'raps' to Spoonerisms, traditional and contemporary nonsense verses and Dr. Seuss.

All this is hardly old-style phonics and 'learning your sounds'. We now have exciting research endorsement of the significance of the poetic, playful and subversive elements in language and these should be celebrated in early years settings and classes. Children can be helped to make up and record – on tape, computer disk and in handmade books – their own rhymes, songs, alliterative chants, nonsense and mini-stories. They can also build up alphabets of their names, or likes and dislikes, or collect sets of names or foods which begin with the same sounds. All this is so much more exciting and cognitively demanding than commercially produced wall charts.

Parents, carers and early years professionals can also take heart from the support which modern research gives to young children's experiments with early writing and inventive spelling. This will be developed in the next chapter, but we can note here the important insights which children gain into the relationship between the sounds and the symbols of a written language, if they are allowed to try out their own theories about writing.

A prerequisite of literacy is some level of awareness on the part of the learner that speaking and writing are different, and that writing is a system for representing most of the sounds of the spoken language, as well as aspects of its rhythms, intonation patterns and ways of expressing ideas and feelings. These complex insights are not beyond young children who have already acquired a language, or two, without direct teaching. Such insights can be nurtured and extended by 'collecting' and talking about language – our differing languages, accents, dialects and varieties like rhyming slang and Caribbean creoles. These are the things that professional linguists do and they call this kind of 'language about language' *metalinguistics*. The National Curriculum now emphasises it as

Language Study in all the three components of the English Orders: speaking and listening, reading, writing. It might also be called playing with sounds and sense and learning to love language.

This discussion should have highlighted the great importance of literature in the early years, particularly that literature which is rooted in the old oral traditions. We need to tell this material to young children, as well as introducing them to the written versions. This means lots of exposure to folk tales, fairy tales, myths, legends, nursery rhymes and ballads, as well as modern reworkings of traditional themes and a wide range of contemporary literature.

Observations and records

We can create our own guidelines for what we need to note about children's early language and literary development using such headings as:

- languages spoken;

- story and narrative responses;

- evidence of play with language;

- familiarity with stories, poetry and rhymes;

- sensitivity to music, rhythm and repetition;

- awareness of alliteration and rhymes in language;

- general interest in how languages work and are different at the levels of words and sounds (as in dialects, accents and pronunciation);

- willingness to draw and write messages and stories and invent spelling patterns;

- knowledge of alphabet letter names and their common sound equivalents;

- knowledge of other writing systems and literacy traditions;

- interest in books and written material of all kinds.

These aspects of development can be written out as lists or observation guidelines, and helpful suggestions for many types of record-keeping can be found in the first book in this series (Bartholomew and Bruce, 1993). Whatever types of records are kept, they must show: the date; preferably the time; the child's name; age in years and months; and the setting or context in which the child's behaviour or response occurred. Some kind of space should also be left for the practitioner's reflections on the significance of the recorded event, behaviour or response, and her plans for following it up with new provision and/or other strategies.

CHOOSING AND USING LITERATURE

This section offers some advice on the important art of storytelling, as distinct from story-reading, in early years settings. It also suggests a few priorities to consider when choosing books for young children and has some comments about the environment in which children are encouraged to enjoy literature. Finally, a list of books to start a collection, or enrich an existing one, is offered – very tentatively.

Storytelling

Much as I love books, I have to admit that good storytelling sessions are magical because no books or pictures come between the listeners and the tale. In early years settings the lifeline between the imaginations of young listeners and the tale is the teller, but good telling is an art which can be perfected. The following hints may help.

A sense of story
The teller must enjoy the story and find it worth telling; a sense of story means understanding the plot, its repeated patterns and its climaxes, its final outcome, as well as the nature of the characters. Language is the heart of any telling and must be enjoyed for its sounds, rhythms and repetitions.

The telling
The voice of the teller must convey the plot, the characters and the moral and emotional propositions of the story by many subtle changes of pitch, volume and pauses. A range of language registers, styles and accents will often be needed to differentiate characters. Eye-contact with the listeners, facial expressions, gestures, body posture and an element of mime are essential to support the teller's words and help the listeners' understanding.

The listeners
Closeness to the teller and reasonable comfort are essential and the traditional storytelling circle, or semi-circle, is probably the best way to achieve them. Participation in the telling should come from joining in with the repeated questions, answers, choruses and refrains found in traditional and modern

tales; sometimes questions and requests for advice, in role, should be directly addressed to the audience, although excessive interruptions from young listeners can be gently postponed until the end of the story (but never forgotten!). Showing objects which relate to the story helps listeners to concentrate (a magic stone, a character's hat). Some traditional storytellers always sit in a special chair, or wear a special hat or shawl, or play a simple musical instrument at the start and the conclusion of a tale.

We can learn from all these techniques, but the secret is to enjoy ourselves. We do not have to be word perfect and learn stories off by heart: the bare bones are all that is needed because the flesh is put on in the telling. We also need to remember that other storytellers can be recruited from among parents, the wider community, especially the elderly, and from older children.

Choosing books

Choosing books for young children is a great responsibility because we are directly influencing the views they will develop about literature, books and reading. The unspoken question is always, what is in it for them? With this in mind I shall merely pick out some priorities which can guide adults who choose mainly fiction books for young children. Detailed reviews of the full range of books published for children are available in specialist journals and should be consulted by early years practitioners. For example, *Books For Keeps*, 6 Brightfield Road, Lee, London, SE12 8QF.

Quality literature

Ensuring that children encounter quality literature will involve us in looking at the language of books, their illustrations and the range of challenges they offer. Quality language includes interesting and unusual words, realistic conversations, humour and ambiguous meanings and a variety of styles.

Illustrations are no longer extra accompaniments to the text in children's books: they may even tell a different story! They usually extend the meanings of the text and, such is the prestige of the picture book, many are works of art in their own right. The significance of the images in a book are now much greater: we live in a world of television, film and computers where children develop sophisticated abilities to read pictures and symbols at an early age.

Quality literature always offers a range of social, emotional and moral challenges and young readers will need to explore, sometimes with an interested adult and sometimes alone, their own thoughts on the new issues they meet in books. They will also need the support and reassurance of familiar well-loved texts which they have made their own.

Equal opportunities

The range of books which we provide for our children should enable all of them to feel at home in the world of literature. Powerful signals about who is 'invisible', who is not competent or who is not valued can be given by the themes, characters, language and illustrations of books. Books are immensely prestigious in a literate culture and particular groups of children, or whole communities, whose existence is not reflected accurately in books may be humiliated and rendered powerless. There is still a long way to go in the provision of quality literature which values all our children, but we can find some books which celebrate the lives of children from many ethnic groups. There are also a number of books with determined and strong females and thoughtful and caring males in them, but few quality books for younger children have central characters with physical and mental disabilities, or working class backgrounds.

'Trash' and choice

Children's books are not usually associated with pulp fiction and romantic trash, but there are still plenty of poorly produced, cheaply illustrated books with predictable and boring plots available for young children. They are found in corner shops, petrol stations, chain stores and supermarkets, sometimes displayed next to books of acknowledged quality. This 'trash' often includes books which claim to be educational, such as very predictable 'A for apple' alphabets, 'counting' and 'colours' books. While not wishing to spend limited resources on this material, I would not rush to condemn it, particularly if parents and carers use it to read with their children and teach them about letters and numbers. Furthermore, children's own book choices should be respected and acknowledged, even if they are not what we would choose. Literary discrimination and a passion for reading are based on a very wide experience of books and other written materials and we all need a bit of trashy reading at times. What do you read in trains and waiting rooms, or on holiday? And who can ever know what deep psychological needs of a young child are met and comforted by 'Topsy and Tim' or some anonymous fluffy bunny story?

The setting

It is not enough to provide the books, read them to the children and have frequent storytelling sessions. Careful thought and organisation must go into the environment in which children hear stories and investigate books.

The right physical environment can help young children to feel good about sitting alone with a book, sharing books with their friends, or settling down in a big group to listen to book-reading and storytelling by an adult. Priority should be given to creating an area which is screened off from potentially messy and boisterous activities; ideally it should be carpeted, have cushions, one or two tables and room for a few pictures, plants and soft toys. Displays of natural objects like stones, shells, seeds and spices or collections of buttons, keys, marbles and even attractive bottles will add to the appeal of the area.

The books should be displayed on tables and low shelves with their attractive covers showing, or open at interesting illustrations. A large, unsorted collection of books can be overwhelming and very unappealing, especially if it is jammed tightly in wire racks and heavy boxes. An early years collection should be small and changed frequently, although especially popular books may never be rested and eventually fall apart with loving use. A good end for any book!

Books should certainly migrate to other parts of the room when they are required to extend a display, provide information about an activity, encourage a new interest or just accompany a young reader on a little walk. There should also be a special place where the children know they can find the books which the adults are currently reading to them. Access to a well-known text helps children retell for themselves a very familiar sequence of pictures, events or words: this activity is another crucial factor in early reading success.

Starting a collection

The following lists are no more than personal choices from a huge range of literature and your own special favourites may well be missing. If my list disappoints, then you are probably a true book-lover and will already be giving the children in your care a literary education.

The selection is grouped into broad categories, or genres, and includes well-known favourites and some newer books. Many of the books would be equally at home in several of the lists: stories written in rhyme, for example, and picture books of traditional material. Picture books appear in all the categories and, along with traditional literature, dominate this selection. The appeal of these kinds of books for the early years should not blind us, however, to their significance for much older readers. I have included a few modern retellings of traditional material which subvert the old themes and even meddle with the conventions of book design.

Traditional literature
Briggs, Raymond, *Jim and the Beanstalk*, Hamish Hamilton, Puffin.
Browne, Anthony, *The Tunnel*, Julia Macrae, Walker.

Carter, Angela, *Sleeping Beauty and Other Favourite Fairy Tales*, Gollancz.

Jaffrey, Madhur, *Seasons of Splendour*, Pavilion, Puffin.

McKissak, Patricia C., *Flossie and the Fox*, Kestrel, Puffin.

Ormerod, Jan, *The Story of Chicken Licken*, Walker.

Patterson, Geoffrey, *The Goose that Laid the Golden Egg*, Deutsch, Picture Piper.

Rosen, Michael, *Hairy Tales and Nursery Crimes*, Young Lions.

Ross, Tony, *Goldilocks and The Three Bears*, Andersen, Sparrow.

Scieszka, Jon, *The Stinky Cheese Man and Other Fairly Stupid Tales*, Puffin.

Scieszka, Jon, *The True Story of The 3 Little Pigs*, Puffin.

Steptoe, John, *Mufaro's Beautiful Daughters*, Hamish Hamilton, Hodder and Stoughton.

Trivizas, Eugene, *The Three little Wolves and the Big Bad Pig*, Heinemann.

Williams, Jay, *The Practical Princess and Other Liberating Fairy Tales*, Nelson, Hippo.

Picture books

Ahlberg, Janet and Allan, *The Jolly Postman*, Heinemann.

Bang, Molly, *Ten, Nine, Eight*, Puffin.

Blake, Quentin, *Quentin Blake's ABC*, Cape.

Burningham, John, *Come Away from the Water, Shirley*, Cape, Picture Lions.

Burningham, John, *Courtney*, Cape.

Butterworth, Nick, *Jasper's Beanstalk*, Hodder and Stoughton.

Cooper, Helen, *The Bear Under the Stairs*, Doubleday, Picture Corgi.

Henderson, Kathy, *In the Middle of the Night*, Walker.

Hughes, Shirley, *Alfie Gets in First*, Bodley Head, Picture Lions.

Kitamura, Satoshi, *When Sheep cannot Sleep*, A and C Black, Beaver.

Lord, John Vernon, *The Giant Jam Sandwich*, Cape.

Macaulay, David, *Black and White*, Houghton Mifflin.

McKee, David, *Not Now, Bernard*, Andersen, Arrow.

Ormerod, Jan, *Sunshine*, Kestrel, Puffin.

Sendak, Maurice, *Where The Wild Things Are*, Bodley Head, Puffin.

Vipont, Elfrida, *The Elephant and the Bad Baby*, Hamish Hamilton, Puffin.

Waddell, Martin, *Can't You Sleep Little Bear?*, Walker.

Walsh, Jill Payton, *Babylon*, Deutsch, Beaver.

Poetry and rhyme

Aardema, Verna, *Bringing the Rain to Kapiti Plain*, Macmillan.

Agard, John, *I Din Do Nuttin*, Bodley Head.

Agard, John and Nichols, Grace (eds.), *A Caribbean Dozen*, Walker.

Ahlberg, Allan, *Please Mrs. Butler*, Kestrel, Puffin.
Ahlberg, Janet and Allan, *Each Peach Pear Plum*, Kestrel, Picture Lions.
Cope, Wendy (ed.), *The Orchard Book of Funny Poems*, Orchard.
Matterson, Elizabeth (ed.), *This Little Puffin*, Puffin.
Opie, Iona (ed.), *Tail Feathers from Mother Goose, The Opie Rhyme Book*, Walker.
Opie, Iona and Peter (eds.), *I Saw Esau. The Schoolchild's Pocket Book*, Walker.
Rosen, Michael, *Quick, Let's Get Out of Here*, Deutsch, Puffin.
Rosen, Michael, *Don't Put Mustard in the Custard*, Deutsch, Puffin.
Stevenson, Robert Louis and Foreman, Michael, *A Child's Garden of Verses*, Gollancz.

Families
Breinburg, Petronella, *My Brother Sean*, Bodley Head, Puffin.
Browne, Anthony, *Gorilla*, Julia Macrae, Little Mammoth.
Browne, Anthony, *Piggybook*, Julia Macrae, Magnet.
Burningham, John, *Avocado Baby*, Cape, Picture Lions.
Edwards, Hazel, *There's a Hippopotamus on our Roof Eating Cake*, Picture Knight.
Gray, Nigel, *I'll Take You to Mrs. Cole*, Picturemac.
Hayes, Sarah, *Eat Up Gemma*, Walker.
Hoffman, Mary, *Amazing Grace*, Frances Lincoln.
Hutchins, Pat, *Titch*, Puffin.
Murphy, Jill, *Five minutes Peace*, Walker.
Murphy, Jill, *Peace at Last*, Macmillan.
Wells, Rosemary, *Noisy Nora*, Collins, Picture Lions.

Animals
Barber, Antonia, *The Mousehole Cat*, Walker.
Burningham, John, *Courtney*, Cape, Puffin.
Felix, Monique, *Another Story of . . . The Little Mouse Trapped in a Book*, Methuen.
Felix, Monique, *The Wind; The House; The Colours*; Stewart, Tabori and Chang/Creative education.
Graham, Amanda, *Arthur*, Puffin.
Hutchins, Pat, *Rosie's Walk*, Bodley Head, Puffin.
King-Smith, Dick, *The Sheep-Pig*, Gollancz, Puffin.
Moore, Inga, *Six Dinner Sid*, Simon and Schuster Young Books.
Simmonds, Posy, *Fred*, Cape, Puffin.
Waddell, Martin, *Farmer Duck*, Walker.

Issues
Ahlberg, Janet and Allan, *Starting School*, Viking Kestrel.
Browne, Anthony, *Zoo*, Julia Macrae, Red Fox.

Burningham, John, *Granpa*, Cape, Puffin.
Burningham, John, *Aldo*, Cape, Puffin.
Cowcher, Helen, *Tigress*, Andre Deutsch.
Keats, Ezra Jack, *Goggles*, Bodley Head, Puffin.
Seuss, Dr. *The Sneetches and other stories*, Collins, London.
Varley, Susan, *Badger's Parting Gifts*, Andersen, Picture Lions.
Wagner, Jenny, *John Brown, Rose and the Midnight Cat*, Kestrel, Puffin.
Wells, Rosemary, *Benjamin and Tulip*, Kestrel, Puffin.

Longer 'reads', collections and series

Brown, Jeff, *Flat Stanley*, Methuen, Mammoth.
Cameron, Ann, *The Julian Stories*, Gollancz, Young Lions.
Dahl, Roald, *The B.F.G.*, Puffin.
Dahl, Roald, *James and the Giant Peach*, Puffin.
Dahl, Roald, *Fantastic Mr. Fox*, Viking, Puffin.
Edwards, Dorothy, *My Naughty Little Sister*, Methuen, Puffin.
Hughes, Ted, *The Iron Man*, Faber.
Leaf, Munro, *The Story of Ferdinand*, Hamish Hamilton, Puffin.
Mark, Jan, *Nothing To Be Afraid Of*, Kestrel, Puffin.
Norton, Mary, *The Borrowers*, Dent, Puffin.
Storr, Catherine, *Clever Polly and the Stupid Wolf*, Faber, Puffin.
Tomlinson, Jill, *The Owl who was Afraid of the Dark*, Methuen, Puffin.
Willis, Jeanne, *Dr Xargle's Book of Earthlets; Dr Xargle's Book of Earth Tiggers*, etc.,
    Andersen, Red Fox.

4 Literacy: The 'Early' Early Years 0–5

The decision to discuss literacy in two chapters, one for the 'early' early years and one for the start of statutory schooling, is not based on some notion that these arrangements are universal and dictated by human development (later starts to compulsory schooling in the rest of the developed world give the lie to such an assumption). In fact, these two chapters assume a continuity of literacy development and experiences in the years from nought to eight and Chapter 5 will make no sense unless it is based on the claims of this chapter. However, literacy is a complex topic and simply in order to manage the discussion it has been divided into an early and a later phase of the years nought to eight. Two positive effects of this decision are the attention it focuses on literacy from birth to five, and locating literacy development and teaching in the five to eight phase within a distinctive early years tradition.

Defining literacy

Most definitions of literacy emphasise the ability to read and write using the conventional system of written signs of a particular language and, of course, individuals can be literate in more than one language. Modern definitions tend to extend this basic notion of literacy to indicate a level of competence which enables the literate individual to function independently and flexibly in a society. We might describe this as emancipatory literacy (Freire and Macedo, 1987), or the appropriate literacy for citizenship in a democracy. This broader definition is a helpful reminder that literacy is not just the main business of schooling, but an aspect of living and coping in a community. Thus it is perfectly reasonable to claim that very young infants discover print and get drawn into the literacy events (Heath, 1983) of their communities long before they meet a teacher. Most educational settings now use the term literacy (in preference to 'reading and writing') in order to avoid any hint of separate activities and tight distinctions in our responses to print. The relationships between producing writing and reading print will become evident in this and the next chapter.

Literacy beyond schooling

It is helpful to think of literacy as a cultural tool which changes the ways in which a language group thinks and gets things done. For example, the very fact that written records exist means that little is forgotten, but it is impossible for any of us to know all of this mass of print. Similarly, children cannot read and recall everything, but they should know how to seek things out. Remember that real readers have the right to choose what they like, or need, to read (Pennac, 1994) and they also have the right to 'skip' irrelevant or unappealing material.

Literate cultures develop an idea of history based on documents, but this evidence is often a source of inconsistencies, scepticism and doubts. In contrast, the old ballads and tales of the oral tradition agreed on who did what, who was wholly good and who was wholly bad, with no written evidence to confuse the issues. Literacy inevitably introduces children to diversity and controversy and requires them to take on differing viewpoints.

Literate societies are never uniform in their acquisition and use of literacy: there are huge variations in the literacy skills and traditions of individuals and groups in any society. These different literacy achievements also divide societies according to who can do what: individuals and groups are judged and pigeon-holed according to the kinds and amounts of reading and writing they do. Literacy is seen by parents and communities as the key to survival and success for their children, and rightly so, but this may put intolerable pressure on early years professionals to push little children into inappropriate reading and writing exercises.

Distinctive kinds of thinking are associated with literacy, in particular the ability to stop and reflect on ideas and events when they are captured in writing. Literacy also promotes 'disembedded' thinking. This is thinking which is free from specific contexts and, therefore, highly theoretical. It is the kind of thinking about thinking used in logic, philosophy and literary theory. These reflective and abstract ways of thinking are highly valued in the later years of formal education, but if children are to develop them eventually, they need time in their early years to think and mull things over and to engage in varied experiences. They need many opportunities to enjoy and investigate meaningful literacy.

Two misunderstandings

There are many misunderstandings about the 'early' early years, including a widespread tendency to believe that little children have little brains, despite modern findings on how much of the brain's potential is mapped out in the first year of life (Carnegie, 1994). Two particular misunderstandings can undermine literacy in the 'early' early years: the notion of 'pre' literacy and the notion of preparatory or basic skills.

Young children's first investigations of print and their first attempts to use written symbols are not 'pre', they are the real thing! These are the earliest stages of literacy and they do involve real reading and real writing. It is much more helpful to think of the emergence of literacy (Hall, 1987) as a lifelong process – we can be involved in it in various ways all our lives. My own struggles to write this book are no different in kind from my eight-year-old granddaughter's efforts to write a ghost story set in a castle she visited, or my five-year-old grandson's attempts to write a postcard to me.

Related to the 'pre' notion is the misleading idea that children must first be taught the so-called basic skills and made to practise and remember them, before they are let loose on real reading and writing. This is as foolish and irrelevant as suggesting that babies should be given preliminary lessons in elocution and syntax before being allowed to try speaking! Highly complex skills are not so easily understood, let alone broken down into easy chunks, practised and then recombined for later use. Misguided attempts to do this with children often lead adults to concentrate totally on the surface bits (like the 'correct' formation of letters and reciting the alphabet) to the neglect of the real literacy basics. The real basics of literacy must include purposes, motives and understanding. Children learn literacy skills in the process of using writing and reading for their own purposes; similarly, the pleasures and the advantages of communicating first launched them into talking.

THE ROOTS OF LITERACY

The roots of literacy in the years before five can only be understood if we are consciously aware that literacy is a sophisticated extension of spoken language. The earlier chapters on language, talk and stories are the crucial underpinning for this discussion. But from this rich mixture of language and social learning in the 'early' early years it is possible to pick out at least two aspects of the young child's development which are the roots of literacy:

- making sense of things;

- symbols, representations and mark-making.

Making sense of things

We can probably agree that all learning comes down to the drive to understand and manage ourselves and our environment. This impels small children to explore and play with all the objects, events and people who come their way: from saucepan lids to peek-a-boo with a shop assistant, and from a puddle to a yoghurt carton. One feature of modern life which comes the child's way and cries out for investigation is the print which covers, literally, every aspect of our environment. Print is everywhere, on clothes and shoes, on all food containers and packaging, on vehicles and domestic appliances, on buildings, road signs and street names, in garages and supermarkets and on toys and baby equipment. None of these is a conventional source of print, like books, newspapers, magazines and correspondence, but if we add these traditional sources of literacy to the endless list of what is often called environmental print we can see that our cultures really do deluge us in print.

None of this is lost on very young children and there is widespread evidence that two-, three- and four-year-olds notice print, ask questions about it and even attempt to create it themselves (Bissex, 1980; Ferreiro and Teberosky, 1982; Newkirk, 1984; Payton, 1984). These young children, observed in their everyday home and group settings around the world, were already asking important literacy questions about print, writing and reading. Questions such as 'what's that?', 'what does that say?', 'how do you write my name?' or 'can you read that?' are familiar to most carers and early years workers. The variations on these are many, but we can summarise this drive to make sense of print as two broad enquiries: 'what is it for?' and 'what is in it for me?'. Similar questions lie behind all the thinking, investigating and play of young infants, from attempts to taste and mouth objects such as fir cones and wooden blocks, to pushing sticks and stones into a drain cover, or finding that a good shake turns a box of cereal into a musical instrument.

Environmental print and books can be very rewarding aspects of children's investigations of their world, particularly if caring and interested adults show enthusiasm for the children's discoveries and demonstrate more uses for books and the print that is everywhere.

Symbols, representations and mark-making

Symbols

The previous section dealt with aspects of thinking which are extended by children's encounters with their social and physical environments. But the infant mind is not an empty vessel just waiting to be filled, even with print and the important sense-making strategies indicated above. The infant mind is, from the start, a finely tuned tool for thinking (Gardner, 1991). This is obvious in the earliest non-verbal communications between babies and carers (see Chapter 1), in the kinds of play and explorations referred to above, in young children's narratives and responses to stories (Chapter 3) and in their earliest making of marks with pens, paint and other media. All these activities are 'part of a family of interrelated expressions and representations' (Matthews, 1994a, p. 31). These representations enable us to select, hold on to, understand and share our emotionally, intellectually and culturally meaningful ideas. They appear to emerge in infancy in many diverse cultures and may be characteristic of the human mind, like language potential (Matthews, 1994b). The family name for these activities is *symbolising* and the family is in the business of *representation*.

We are all 'awash in a sea of symbols' (Gardner, 1991), symbols which enable us to communicate with each other, become part of a cultural group and also express our uniquely personal inner worlds and thoughts. Symbols include all the cultural systems like language, numbers and print; pictures, icons, codes of dress and traffic signals; games, buildings, religious rituals and rules for social events and personal contacts. Symbols can also be highly personal, ranging from dreams and gestures to strong attachments to particular soft toys, blankets, songs and pieces of music, vehicles, and even places. What do these endless and infinitely variable lists have in common? What makes them symbols and not just references to piles of masonry, scraps of fabric or haphazard noises and marks? The simple answer is that they are a focus for our feelings and stand for, or represent, whole sequences of human emotions, thoughts, experiences and cultural beliefs.

Representations

Symbols work by representation; they are generalised thoughts about life and experience and make all forms of communication possible. It is widely accepted that infants are born with an ability to understand actions and objects and other human beings, and they treat these categories of things differently (see Chapter 1). All later representations are derived from this important 'starter-pack' for thinking. The pattern of these developments is complex and not easily described, but the general view is that the infant's earliest experiences of actions, movements and images are retained by the brain, or internalised, thus creating sets of general expectations about experience. We might understand these as thoughts, or representations, about people and things. This representational thinking is well established when a child 'recognises', or literally 're-thinks', a cat pictured on a pet food label. She may point to it, name it, say 'miaow' or even set off to look for the family pet, or a toy cat, or a picture of a cat in a book. This example shows that representations enable us to think about and recall things and people in their absence and make connections between similar events, images and objects. But representations can also be played with and used to extend our thinking. A child of 18 months need not stop at saying 'miaow', she may climb into the cat's basket, pretend to scratch her carer, and even experiment with eating from the cat's bowl! Significantly for this discussion, this small child can also make her own marks on paper, or other surfaces, and label them as 'cat'.

Mark-making

Mark-making involves both creativity, communication and some degree of permanence; these are important components of literacy. We talk quite easily of someone making their mark in the world, but forget that it is a metaphor recalling the simple cross which stands for the signature of a person who is illiterate. And this mark is essentially like the first mark an infant may produce by dragging a chocolate-covered finger across a wall or table surface. A mark which did not exist in the world has been created, it remains as a trace of an action, and communicates the message that someone was here. The mark of the illiterate adult is made intentionally, but it too symbolises personal existence and communicates an understanding of some transaction. The first marks of the infant may begin as accidents, but they also record existence and are the start of a long process in which the happy accident of a chocolate mark, or a damp patch, stimulates many repeat performances with a variety of markers and surfaces (Matthews, 1994a). The activity of mark-making has its own inner drive or developmental programme, but it also coincides with, and is strengthened by, encounters with the print systems of the immediate culture and the huge admiration of caring adults. In these very early days of literacy the representation of movement, space, shape and emotions, which we call drawing, also includes the making of marks which are more like letters and numerals. This is an important reminder that writing emerges from drawing (figure 4), is often inspired by drawing, and can be sustained by it throughout the years of schooling – and long after.

BECOMING A WRITER

Becoming literate in the earliest years is bound up with trying to behave like a reader and a writer and gradually getting the pretending closer and closer to the real thing. Playing and investigating are, therefore, very significant activities for the emerging reader and writer. We will follow the path taken by many young children around the world and start with writing first.

Figure 4   Writing emerges from mark-making and drawing

Investigating print

Any investigation involves careful observations. Young Cushla is fascinated by the calendar in her grandmother's kitchen:

> *. . . on being held close she would make a strenuous effort to focus on the large black numbers underneath the coloured picture. She would then appear to 'scan' them, the whole procedure occupying several minutes.*
> (Butler, 1979, p. 26)

Cushla was eight months old at the time. Furthermore, she was so frail and genetically impaired that she could have been classed as seriously retarded, a hopeless case. Indeed, her successful development through the sharing of books is a very special case, but it does remind us that we may underestimate young infants' fascination with print. Very young children are more likely to investigate print and learn about it if three important conditions are met:

- the print is genuine;

- the situation supports play;

- the method is scientific.

This may sound rather grand for the years before five, but it is based on substantial evidence of how such young children successfully get into print. 'The print is genuine' is a reminder that young children cannot become entranced by a kitchen calendar or the bold black letter 'b' in a picture alphabet book (Butler, 1979, p. 27) unless they come across such things and are allowed to indulge their attachment to them. Genuine print is everywhere and we do not need to look for specially prepared and 'gimmicky' material for our youngest children. I know several two- and three-year-old collectors of catalogues, holiday brochures and used greetings cards who refer to this material as their 'books'. I also know some very young 'writers' who can empty the official forms and advisory leaflets racks of their local post office or bank with embarrassing speed and complete all the relevant sections! These children are telling us that they wish to join the literacy club too (Smith, 1988) and they intend to find out what all this print does for people (figure 5). However, they cannot ask questions about what print is for if we regularly force them to engage with

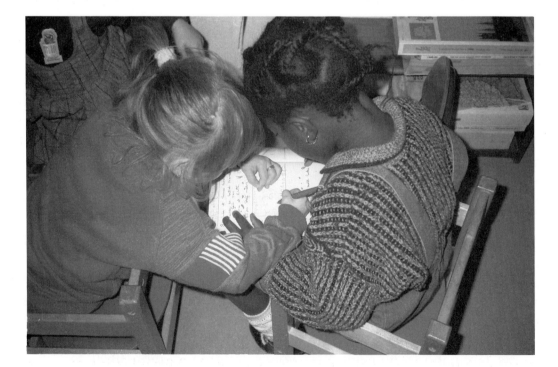

Figure 5   Four-year-olds filling in their appointments diary

bits of print that are not for anything or anyone, except 'early learning'. Sophisticated computer software which promises to 'teach your kids, ages three to five' the alphabet, phonics, reading readiness and spelling should be viewed critically. It may well be taking children further away from all the activities and investigations with real print in their community which they need in order to make sense of letters, sounds and spelling patterns.

'The situation supports play' is a serious point about young children's approaches to investigating print and indicates the attitudes and atmosphere which should prevail when very young children look at print and make their own marks. Young children play the roles of writers and readers when they explore print and they need to have settings and carers who positively value this and make it possible to play at reading and writing. This means taking seriously what children are doing and asking about, but never suggesting that their mistakes, misunderstandings and wild inventions are serious offences which will be mocked or punished. The children's literacy explorations are play because they are done for their own sake, the activities are their own reward. They are play activities because they have a protected status: they are safe from demands to conform to agendas imposed by people external to the play. In the case of literacy, or any other objects, situations or materials children choose to play with, there are constraints set by the material itself. These intrinsic demands and the motivation to explore them make play a significant way of learning.

'The method is scientific' refers to young children's learning and highlights the way in which they investigate print and the kinds of help they will need. When faced with something new but not too threatening, children behave like scientists and make up a story, a hypothesis, about what it is and what it means. 'That says Smarties' a four-year-old tells me, pointing to the logo and picture on the front of a box, although he is accustomed to getting these sweets in a handy tube. On this occasion his explanatory story is correct, he has made the right links with previous experience and my feedback confirms his hypothesis. Feedback about how well a hypothesis works is essential to scientists, young and old, but if children are to act like readers and writers they also need models to copy and demonstrations of how it is done. This need not be daunting or like formal school lessons; it simply means involving young children in the kinds of writing and reading which we have to do anyway. Little children can add their marks to shopping lists, put kisses and 'messages' on letters, notes and cards, 'sign' their names on their belongings, fill in spare forms from shops, catalogues and offices and write letters to put in used envelopes (figure 6). Sharing everyday literacy with small children has an added bonus for adults – it is fun and it can be extended to other non-literacy activities. Children can be

Figure 6   An envelope addressed to Granny and Grandad (four years five months)

Figure 7   Mark-making in the sand (three- and four-year-olds)

encouraged to make their mark on home-made biscuits, pastry and sweets; dry surfaces can be marked with wet hands or brushes; damp sand is an irresistible invitation to mark-makers of all ages (figure 7), and writing and drawing on dry earth with a stick has a long history in many cultures. Children want to make marks, as every carer finds out, but they also need to see the people around them making those significant marks which we call writing.

Children's strategies

Modern views of early childhood emphasise the active and exploratory nature of infant behaviour (Bruner and Haste, 1987; Bennett, 1993) and this is particularly evident in the acquisition of language and in the emergence of early literacy (Whitehead, 1985; Hall, 1987). Children appear to evolve strategies for finding out how literacy works and for getting a grip on the system. The strategies which follow are an attempt to highlight some creative approaches used by young children; *they are not a checklist for testing little children*. On the contrary, they are a starting point for early years carers and professionals to monitor their own understanding of early literacy and their own ability to respond appropriately to what their children are doing.

Ask questions
The most obvious way in which children investigate print has already been noted – they ask direct questions:

> *What does that say?*
> *How do you write 'D' for Daniel?*

If this strategy is to extend the children's understanding they require, and deserve, direct answers to their questions from adults, or older children, and demonstrations of how it is done.

Watch the others
Observing what other people do has also been mentioned above, but there is evidence that very young children who appear to be scribbling wildly are often imitating the speed and fluency of the cursive writing they see adults doing (Whitehead, 1985). They also reproduce the 'spikes and circles' look of writing, as well as its arrangement in lines and its directional flow. These characteristics will reflect those of the particular culture, or cultures, in which any child is observing print and writing activities. Children will also notice and try out some of the very special uses of writing in their cultures. I include one example in which 'watching the others' led a four-year-old who was attending a college

lecture with her mother to write an A4 side of 'lecture notes'. There is one standard word half-way down this page of notes – the child's first name (figure 8).

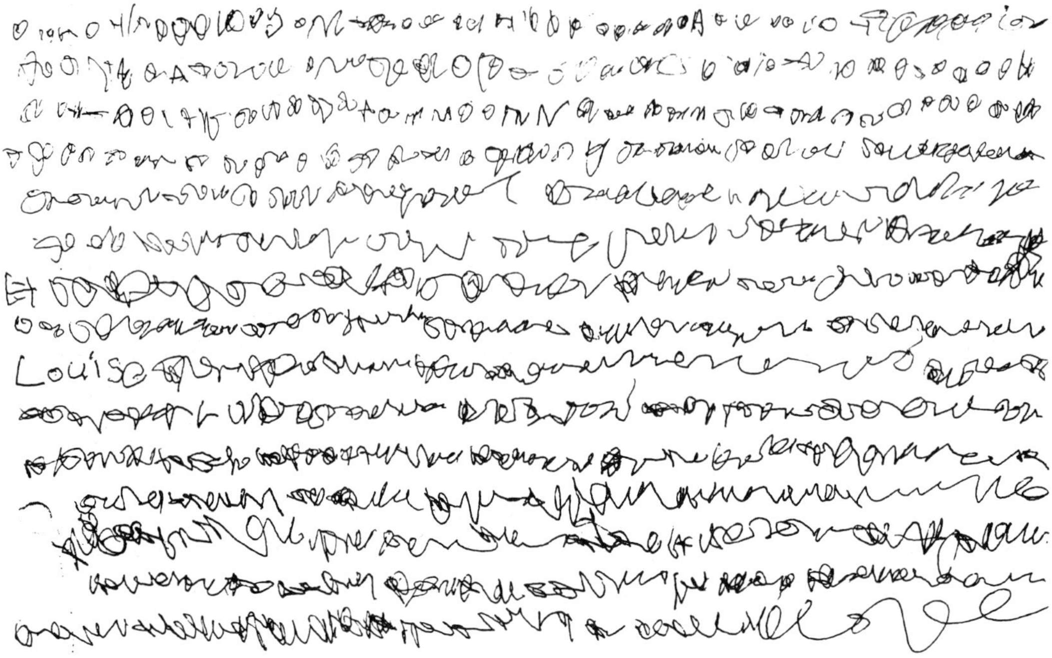

Figure 8   Writing lecture notes in college: four-year-old Louise

Use your name

Our own names are full of meaning for us; they reflect our self-esteem and sense of place in the world. For small children they are often the first words adults help them to write, but they soon have a place in early literacy which goes beyond their important function as a 'me' label. Personal names are the first sets of known sound and symbol combinations with which children feel totally confident. This gives them some very powerful insights into the nature of the written language system.

The initial letters of names become very interesting:

I begin with C (Payton, 1984, p. 85)
That's D for Daniel (pointing to a dinosaur poster)

Other letters from their names begin to be noticed by young children:

I've got one of those in my name (nursery child pointing to the 'M' pendant I was wearing).

Similar letter identifications have been observed by many early years students who take children shopping and encourage them to look closely at the writing on packaging. Close observations of children's paintings, drawings and messages also indicate the presence of personal initials and names. This special knowledge of some significant letters and the sounds they represent is a major breakthrough into literacy and its crucial system of relationships between signs (graphics) and meaningful sounds (phonemes). Knowing how to write your name can also be useful in other ways.

Exploit what you know

This is a very important strategy for the small and powerless who need to join the literacy club. For many young writers, knowing their name is in itself a very useful message; it can say 'here I am' or 'hallo' or 'this is mine'. Many young children get started as letter writers by putting their name on a sheet of paper and filling in the rest of the space with 'kisses' and letter-like shapes (figure 9). The young emergent writer's theory of 'exploit what you know' may be summed up as use what you do know and have a temporary pretend go at the unknown bits. This is a very powerful theory because it enables children to keep on communicating while increasing their hold over more and more pieces of the system.

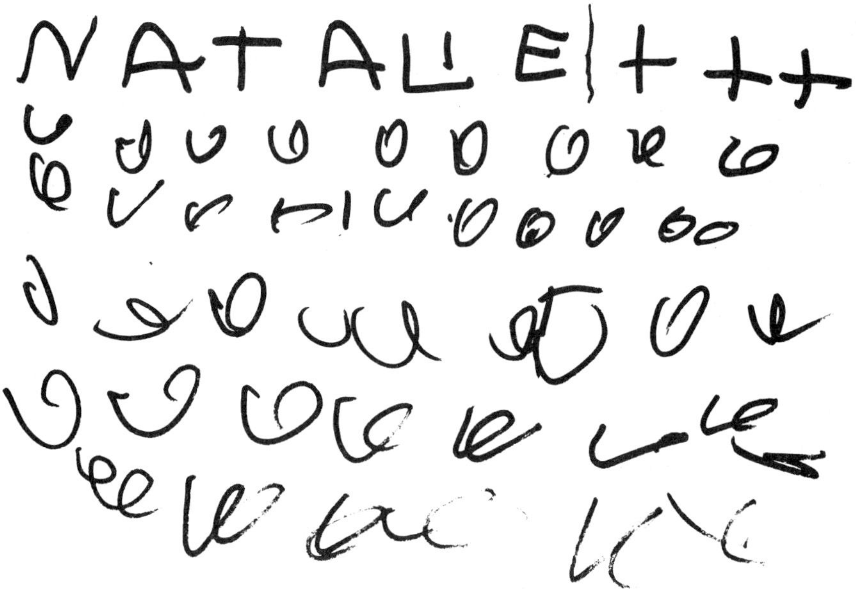

Figure 9   Child's name and early writing (three years six months)

Use alphabets and sounds

Young children may take great pleasure in the alphabets which are so traditional a part of literacy learning in literate cultures (Heath, 1983) and even draw their own 'A for apple' lists (figure 10). This interest in letters and sounds can also be linked with children's apparently instinctive delight in language play and nonsense (Chukovsky, 1963; Whitehead, 1995). Exposure to rhymes, songs, poetry, chants, raps and alphabets can enable children to form some early hypotheses and insights about how written signs represent some of the sounds of speech. This breakthrough can be quite dramatic, as when Daniel (four years nine months) began to point to objects in the room and parts of our bodies and demanded 'What's it start with?'. All these initial letters were written down and as they accumulated I was told to 'read them'. This was a difficult procedure which became ever more hilarious as nonsense sounds and some accidental near-words and rude noises emerged! Our play with the sounds of language and the identification of initial sounds was far more informative for Daniel than any number of classroom 'sound tables' or letter and sound worksheets. In fact, Daniel proudly told all the family that we had invented a language; in a sense we had.

   Children who feel happy to muck about with language and writing begin to

Figure 10   An ABC drawn by a young bilingual (four years six months)

find out that the continuous stream of spoken sound must be broken up into separate words and that similar sounding words, or rhymes, will look similar in some respects when written down.

Many young children discover that the names of letters do suggest speech sounds and syllables and begin to write their own messages in a semi-phonetic code: RUDF (are you deaf) (Bissex, 1980, p. 3). This same child also developed another common early literacy hypothesis: words still communicate very effectively if only consonants are written, as in DSTRB (disturb), or NMBR (number). British children also come up with such examples as FTBL (football) and TBL (table). The important discovery here is that the easily heard consonants and their distinctive patterns are more helpful for word identification than vowels. This system of writing consonants only is used by some modern languages; Hebrew, for example.

Provision and experiences

In the years before five, children need all the rich diversity of a developmentally appropriate early years curriculum which emphasises play, language and investigations in a context of adult support (Bruce, 1987; Athey, 1990; Lally, 1991; Nutbrown, 1994). Early literacy development will be fostered by this broad approach and will require:

- other people who read and write;

- materials for mark-making and writing;

- places set aside for it (in group settings).

The previous discussion has emphasised the crucial role played by the people around young children in modelling what writing is for and how it is done. These people who read and write in order to manage their own lives are the children's first literacy teachers and include parents, carers, siblings, professional teachers and other workers. In home and group settings these important people are readers and scribes for young children and introduce them to the 'ways with words' (Heath, 1983) of their family, community and wider society. It is important that the people around very young children use literacy in all its diversity of styles and purposes and are happy to share the fun of it with the children.

We need to teach one clear lesson: writing is for real purposes which matter to people and it communicates important messages.

Materials for mark-making and writing seems like another fairly obvious requirement, but it bears repeating. This is not simply because without these materials children will have difficulty in developing their interest in, and knowledge about, marks, signs and letters. It is because the variety and range of materials also stimulate new investigations of the possibilities of movements, actions with different markers, use of space and direction and so on (Matthews, 1994a), as well as specific cultural conventions like writing shopping lists and letters. This indicates that a great variety of materials and markers is required. Young children may enjoy thick brushes, chubby crayons and fat felt markers, but they also love to write and draw with biros, fine pencils and thin markers and brushes. Similarly, they need to encounter a range of sizes, textures and colours of paper and card, plus those important oddments which come from real-life literacy such as headed paper, diaries, invitations, greetings cards, calendars, computer print-outs, receipts, menus, bills and programmes of all kinds. The print on these materials is itself a further stimulus to investigate print and its uses and offers more models to copy.

It is important that writing has a special place set aside for it in any group setting, although I would also expect literacy to permeate every corner of a nursery, playgroup or other kind of early years setting, including the outdoor areas. There should be blank shopping lists, telephone message pads, calendars, magazines and newspapers in the home play area (figure 11); patient records, prescriptions and temperature charts in a hospital; plant labels in the garden; recipes and food packages in the kitchen; and the children's own seating plans and 'written' place-setting labels for meals and snacks. A special place for writing can be a corner (figure 12), a group of tables, a table and a low shelf unit, or what you will (figure 13). It should be away from particularly busy pathways and doors and not too close to blockplay or an exciting role-play area, although it will be a place for talking and reading aloud. The writing area signals to the children, as well as to workers, visitors and families, that finding out about print and doing it yourself has a high priority in the early years; it is not something that waits to be taught in the statutory schooling phase. The emphasis must be on the children's active involvement and enjoyment and not on set 'lessons' in copying writing, the correct formation of letters and narrow objectives like learning to write names. Children will do these things anyway, but in the process of more exciting and meaningful tasks like writing down the names of their favourite storybook characters, or marking their personal property. A concern for letter formation in the 'early' early years is best answered by varied provision for drawing, painting, modelling, constructing and mark-making in sand, mud and finger-paint. The writing area may be close to the book collection and it can extend this traditional provision for literature

Figure 11   Leaving messages: four-year-olds in the home play area of a nursery

Figure 12   A special place for writing

Figure 13 Writing area, Comet Nursery School, Hackney

Figure 14 Reading a local street map in the nursery

by providing other literacies such as maps, street directories (figure 14), magazines and comics. Printing sets, typewriters and materials for making simple folded books have a part to play in supporting the investigations of young emergent writers. The availability of computers with basic word processing programs and simple word and picture keyboard overlays should be kept in mind for young children.

BECOMING A READER

Young children investigating print and beginning to write are learning an enormous amount about reading, as the above discussion of their developing alphabetic knowledge has indicated. The purpose of this section is to set out some approaches which are helpful for supporting beginner readers in the years before five, in home and group settings. These approaches can be summarised as:

- you're never too young;

- sharing the pleasure;

- books, tapes and props.

'You're never too young'

This claim refers to the age of the child 'reader', but it has a companion slogan which applies to the parent or carer: 'you don't have to be a teacher of reading'. These ideas are supported by a considerable body of research about successful early reading which goes back many years (White, 1954; Clark, 1976; Butler, 1979; Payton, 1984; Cochran-Smith, 1984) and would include all the evidence from projects which have involved parents and carers in supporting their children's early reading (Weinberger *et al.*, 1991; Wade and Moore, 1993a). Some of the children in these studies were literally babes in arms and the teaching method was a simple matter of sharing picture books with the infants when they were awake and ready to play and socialise. But the phrase 'a simple matter' is misleading because great sensitivity to the baby is required, including a willingness to be guided and paced by her interest and responses. Babies and older toddlers respond to pictures and to print in books in a variety of ways; at first with eye-gaze, smiles, gurgles, squeals, scratching at the paper, pointing and bouncing with enthusiasm. Eventually this develops into naming, joining in with the words, turning the pages and initiating real discussions about characters, motives and plots, as well as linguistic talk about letters, sounds and the conventions of print. The setting in which this can happen must be close, affectionate, enjoyable and relaxed; it can only be achieved in group settings if it is given the very highest priority by highly trained staff.

Sharing the pleasure

Early reading is a partnership of mutual pleasure. It involves the older and wiser partner in taking on as much of the task as is necessary, but always making opportunities for the younger and less experienced child partner to contribute something. Perhaps to touch the page, smile, slot in an appropriate sound-effect, name a character, or join in a repeated phrase or chorus.

Reading the pictures in a book and predicting what is likely to happen can be a first big step forward for a child. This is helped if the adult encourages careful scanning of pictures by talking about them and raising little queries such as 'who is in the boat now?', 'is Little Bear trying to sleep?' or 'what is Gemma eating?'. Of course this must be a subtle and sparingly used ploy, not a page by page inquisition! But gradually the young reader will begin to unpack the layers of meaning and the extra information carried by the pictures in a familiar book. Familiarity is an important point because successful picture reading depends on many re-readings, as I find out whenever I share books with young experts. Did you know that Bernard, of 'not now' fame, has an Elmer book on his bedroom shelf? A four-year-old in a nursery school pointed that out to me recently.

Hearing print brought to life by a familiar voice is another very significant reading lesson and supports young children's awareness of the sound system of the language and its relationship with the written symbols. Sitting comfortably on a lap or very close to a caring adult, the child can both see a meaningful name like 'Fat Cat' (Kent), hear it voiced and pick up on its pleasurable rhyming sounds. This is an example of the roots of early phonological awareness discussed in Chapter 3 and it is supported by all the nursery rhymes, nonsense verses, tongue-twisters, poems and songs we can think of to share with our young reading partners. In the course of these hugely enjoyable activities we will be helping children to learn about initial sounds, the rhymes at the ends of words, and the possible sound substitutions which turn known words into new words. A sequence like 'fat, cat, mat, hat, sat, pat' can be daft, amusing and informative, as the Dr. Seuss books have shown. A substantial experience of music and dance will also contribute to children's enjoyment of rhythms and sounds, while exposure to, and knowledge of, other languages will be helpful in sharpening their general awareness of language and sound.

Close looks at print are an essential part of sharing and reading books in the early years. Evidence that some infants are fascinated by bold print has already been noted (Butler, 1979) and researchers have found that many three- and four-year-olds understand the significance of the print in books (Hall, 1987; Scrivens, 1995). But I am convinced that this interest in the forms of print needs careful nurturing through book sharing and other activities. This is where the creation of a print-rich early years setting (Hall, 1987) is so important, a setting in which all the possible uses of print are exploited to the full. Play areas should contain relevant print so that children encounter the literacies of shops, offices, clinics, gardens and homes, and even get involved in some of the essential literacy of running an early years group setting. Collections of environmental print will enable children to examine, cut up and copy all the distinctive print with which they are familiar and ordinary walks and shopping trips offer many opportunities to examine packaging, street signs and advertisements.

In one-to-one and small group sessions with books, children can be shown significant words such as characters' names, or emotionally powerful words like love, kiss, sad and angry. They can have their attention drawn to initial letters and sounds, especially ones which are also found in their own names, or the names of carers, pets, favourite animals, or film and TV characters. Words which are repeated regularly can be indicated so that the children begin to pick them out and read them. This is a reminder that enjoyable choruses and the repetition of key phrases in children's books are an aid to word recognition, as well as a satisfying literary device. The pointless repetition of reading scheme phrases like 'see, John, see' are not necessary when we have the fun of 'Rumpeta, Rumpeta' (Vipont) or 'Can't you sleep, Little Bear?' (Waddell).

A well-known favourite book is a pleasure for both adult and child reading partners and it is a valuable aid for the beginner reader. Many carers and early years workers are inclined to apologise for a child knowing the text of a book 'off by heart', as if it was a kind of cheating and certainly not to be counted as reading. In fact, it is more helpful to see this achievement as another reading breakthrough. The little child who knows every page of a Spot book (Hill) and 'reads' it has an internal model in her mind of the book and is beginning to match the story and the words in her head to the pages of the book. This skill will enable her to read similar books such as more Spot adventures or other 'lift the flap' books, and gradually focus on the patterns and features of the printed words, because she already knows what meanings they are carrying.

Books, tapes and props

The importance of the provision of books for young children cannot be over-emphasised and the previous chapter and much of this one have made the point again and again. However, two further aspects of book provision should be mentioned: the making of simple books with children and the reading of 'big books'. It is now possible to obtain very large versions of some of the most popular children's books. These are based on the notion that sharing the reading of a book with a group of children enables them to share their literary knowledge with each other and experience all the motivating effects of a shared pleasure. The big book is designed to be shared with a group (Holdaway, 1979) and its size ensures that every child can see the pictures and the print clearly. This means that the adult reading with several children can draw their attention to all the fine details of the print and the pictures, just as in one-to-one readings with a conventional size book (see Chapter 5).

Many young children discover for themselves how to make a book: they fold one or two sheets of paper in half, write and draw on the pages and call it their book (figure 15). This is an indicator of how powerful it is to be a young author and have a book which is unique, and many educators incorporate the making of books with children of all ages into their teaching of reading programmes (Smith, 1994). This activity will be returned to in Chapter 5, but it should certainly start in the pre-school years because making books teaches children about how books work: their pictures and print, the layout of pages, the language of books, and the special language about books (authors, covers, pages, words). The use of photographs can add a personal dimension to a book about a child, a group of children, an outing or a particular setting. The construction can be simple folded sheets, or using the plastic presentation folders sold by stationers, or simply mounted pictures and writing on a folding 'zig-zag' of thin card.

Tapes of favourite stories are now widely available and children find them utterly absorbing. This is because they provide another kind of reading partner, one who never gets bored or tired with telling the same tale over and over. Listening to a tape allows children to match spoken sounds to the words on the page in front of them. This highly motivating experience can be built on by carers and early years professionals if they make extra tapes of themselves telling and reading some of the children's favourite stories, books, rhymes, songs and poems. There is something very special about hearing a familiar voice reading and singing on tape.

Props which support books and stories are not widely known about in the world outside professional early years circles, yet they are becoming a major focus of interest in the field of early literacy. Story props are devices which support the narratives found in books and help young children to remember, retell and extend them. A prop can be a taped version of a book, as discussed above, but it is more likely to be a set of simple reproduction drawings of some

Figure 15   A nursery child making tiny books for a miniature classroom play setting

of the characters in the book, backed with velcro or magnetic tape, so that they can be moved about on a metal or fabric-covered board. Playing with these cut-outs the children are able to reconstruct the shape and the language of the story (figure 16). Sometimes a soft toy can be a story prop and represent the main character, as with a toy Spot, a teddy bear or a 'Lollopy' bunny (Dunbar). This is a particularly interesting type of prop because the child can also tell the story to the toy and take on the role of the more competent partner in the reading partnership. Another kind of prop for playing out and expanding stories can be objects which are similar to those mentioned in the books and stories enjoyed by the children; for example, wooden spoons and cereal bowls (*Goldilocks and the Three Bears*), a shopping basket (*The Shopping Basket*), some hot water bottles (*Phoebe and the Hot Water Bottles*), or a comfort blanket (*Geraldine's Blanket*). All

Figure 16   Nursery children using their own story props for Where The Wild Things Are

these story props are like 'hooks' on which children can hang their retellings of the stories in their books: they are enjoyable ways of playing with books and taking over their narratives.

Early literacy health warnings

Many four-year-old children will not be in early years settings and their early literacy experiences may not be like the approaches described above. These children may be in reception, or mixed age classes, in which case they may be forced to cope with an over-crowded curriculum of ten subjects and denied the intimate close contact with adults which underpins successful literacy partnerships. This all too common situation will endanger young children's literacy development and restrict their learning. The approaches described in this chapter should be available for all young children and we are deluding ourselves and failing our four-year-olds if we rush them into formal schooling in the hope of giving them a good start (EYCG, 1995). An early years setting should be a workshop where young children and adults think, talk and represent their experiences in many ways: by talking, dancing, telling tales, painting, climbing, cooking, building, singing, role-playing and counting. In the process of doing these important things young children become more literate; without these opportunities they are less literate.

We are now at the start of a new era in early childhood education, one in which the curriculum for our four-year-olds is set down in terms of six 'desirable outcomes', or goals, to be reached by the age of five (SCAA, 1996). Some dangerous trends for literacy learning and teaching should be noted.

- Literacy is given a major emphasis but there are some unexplained and unhelpful references to acquiring competence in English 'as soon as possible', listening attentively and handling books carefully. There is little focus on supporting children's growth in self-esteem (Roberts, 1995) or their competence in any language.

- There is no indication that speaking and writing English is not necessarily the first and most appropriate achievement for many children. At four years my granddaughter was writing her name right-to-left in modern Hebrew script in an Israeli kindergarten and also signing her name in left-to-right English script on her mother's letters.

- The general approach underestimates young children's social, cognitive and linguistic abilities and is full of low-level expectations and narrow objectives for early literacy: just naming letters and writing in upper and lower case forms, for example.

- This approach will lead to a 'lowest common denominator' kind of provision and teaching, opening the way for limited instruction in skills for literacy, particularly by untrained and unsupported staff. We may well find an increase in group lessons in 'correct pencil grip', 'correct letter formation' and 'name-writing practice'.

Some of these activities do, of course, have a place in supporting the literacy of groups and individuals, but they can only be effective in contexts which make human and linguistic sense to young children.

5 Literacy: Developing In School 4–8

It is with some reluctance that I define the age-phase of this chapter on literacy in statutory schooling as starting at four, but in recognising the actual situation of many four-year-olds in Britain I also strengthen my claim that literacy learning and teaching in this phase must remain part of a distinctive early years tradition. The early years of statutory schooling cover what we have always called reception, plus Key Stage 1 and the start of Key Stage 2 of the National Curriculum. This mismatch between the well-established international definition of the early years (nought, or three, to eight) and the current education legislation in England and Wales does not necessarily stifle what can be achieved with, and by, four- to eight-year-olds. The situation is a challenge to all of us to demonstrate our understanding of the broad principles which were discussed in Chapter 4, as well as our ability and determination to put them into practice. All early years practitioners, workers and carers can get involved in literacy in some way:

- parents and other carers should demand appropriate language and literacy experiences and teaching for their young children;

- teachers, workers and other professionals should plan the language curriculum according to the ages and stages of the children and the known facts about language and thinking, while also keeping an informed eye on the National Curriculum statutory requirements.

However, we also need to be quite clear that all reception children and all four-year-olds in maintained schools are *not* required to fulfil the Key Stage 1 statutory requirements. Literacy in the early years of schooling is still a matter of building on, developing and extending young children's emerging and quite considerable skills as speakers, listeners, writers and readers. We are more likely to be underestimating children's potential as language learners and limiting their development if we go for the early delivery of any kind of English curriculum which is not based on the principles and concerns discussed in this book, that is:

- talk, stories and narrative;

- making sense of experiences;

- understanding symbols and representations.

There is nothing in these principles which necessarily conflicts with the broad requirements of the National Curriculum. These are the true 'basics' of language and their neglect will certainly undermine the attainments looked for at the end of Key Stages 1 and 2. Effective literacy teaching in the early years of compulsory schooling is dependent on understanding these basic principles and then making them our classroom priorities. This chapter will focus on such priorities and their implications for our work with young children, firstly by providing a checklist for teachers and other adults working in schools, then by discussing the creation of a classroom literacy workshop and, finally, the role of the literacy teacher.

A LANGUAGE TEACHER'S CHECKLIST

All teachers of young children are teachers of language and this list of questions is only a 'starter' for concentrating our minds on the essentials of language and literacy in early years classes. It is not the kind of checklist which only requires ticks in boxes: literacy is never that straightforward!

The setting

— Does the appearance of your room, or setting, or institution, along with its general organisation, kinds of provision and the activities promoted, give the message that you are nurturing and extending a community of speakers and listeners, readers and writers?

Speaking and listening

— Are there ample opportunities and materials for provoking and supporting speaking and listening in the setting?

— Do the children have opportunities to listen to audio-taped stories and poetry – in groups and on individual headsets?

— Do you sometimes provide instructions, guidance and assignments on audio tape?

— Do you all regularly listen to music, recorded and live, in your room or setting?

— Do you and the children sing and recite poems and rhymes frequently?

— Do you take groups of children out on 'listening walks' with a tape recorder and collect interesting daily sounds to use for classroom games of identification and as inspiration for creating songs, poems, stories, paintings, models and dances?

— Do you introduce the children to games which rely on speaking and listening?

— Do you provide some of the stimulus and the all-important approval for the children's role play?

— Do you develop and value drama as a major form of learning in the classroom?

— Are the children helped to make simple puppets and puppet theatres in order to extend their language registers?

— Do you value and develop story*telling*, your own and the children's?

— Do you make story props to support your storytelling, as well as the children's retelling of stories from their favourite books? Do you enable the children to make props for their own invented stories?

— Do you make time for regular daily discussions and for friendly gossip; for verbal planning of play and work with and by the children; for the recall and evaluation of the children's activities and experiences?

— Have the children learnt how to tape interviews with staff, visitors, their families and other children? Do they have opportunities for talk with many different people?

Literature

— Have you created an attractive and welcoming book corner or area? Is the book area lively and interesting, with arrangements of plants, objects, pictures and books?

— Do you locate most of your storytelling and reading with the children here?

— Do you sometimes have a thematic focus on, for example, animals, fairy tales, favourite authors/illustrators, reference books or poetry?

— Are books also displayed in other areas of the room and the setting; near relevant displays, objects, collections and other curriculum areas, for example?

— Have some reference and information books been carefully chosen and made available? Are these used and linked to the children's work and interests? Have you made a start on teaching study skills such as looking things up in a list of contents and an index, or learning to read diagrams, plans and lists?

Literacy

— Is there ample evidence of spontaneous drawing (figure 17) and writing, reading, browsing and sharing of books?

— Are reading and sharing stories and poetry at the heart of your curriculum, or just time-fillers and end of the day pacifiers, or even punishments for difficult groups and individuals?

— Do you and the children use story props, books and audio tapes together?

— Is the making of books at the centre of your literacy teaching and the children's literacy learning?

— How can you raise the literacy profile of other curriculum and play provision areas? Are there, for instance, newspapers, comics, magazines; notebooks, pads of blank paper, paper for lists; pencils, crayons and pens; notices, guidelines and instructions in such places as maths tables, science areas, home corners and role play and brick play areas?

— Do curriculum subjects such as science, PE, music and religious studies inspire reading and writing?

— How varied is the drawing and writing in your room (figure 18)? Have you a class message board and can children and their families contribute? Do the youngest children have a well-positioned chalk-board or flip-chart on which they can make marks and scribble boldly?

— Do you have an attractive and well-maintained writing area, table, or corner with a range of markers, papers, erasers, etc?

— Do you regularly display examples of scripts from different cultures; written messages and information in other languages; illuminated letters, various alphabets, varied writing patterns and styles?

— Do you help the children to collect and display environmental print and do you provide photographs of signs and familiar logos?

— Is there an exciting collection of letters, newsprint, postcards, recipes,

Figure 17　*'My favourite animal at the farm was Martha the pig' (five years), reception class, South London*

Figure 18　*A picture of Robin Hood (five years one month), reception class, South Wales*

greetings cards, invitations, official forms and packaging for the children to read, use, or cut up and recycle?

—   What word resources are there in the room and the setting? Are there lists of words and phrases which the children use regularly? Are there collections of words accompanying displays and materials? Are there useful labels and name cards around the room? Do you involve the children in discussing, placing and making use of these kinds of labels?

—   Do you play daily games with sounds, rhymes, tongue-twisters and verbal nonsense?

—   Do you help the children to invent their own alphabets and playfully build up word families (sun, fun, run, etc.)?

—   Do you plan for frequent sessions of shared reading and writing in large and small groups, as appropriate?

—   Do you and other adults maximise your literacy usefulness to the children? Are you acting as secretaries, scribes, typists, computer-operators, proof-readers, authors, publishers and correspondents for the children?

The rest of this chapter will develop some of the issues raised by the language teacher's checklist.

THE LITERACY WORKSHOP

An early years classroom or setting which is organised as a literacy workshop has two important characteristics: one 'practical' and the other I can describe as 'philosophical/motivational'.

The practical essence of a workshop is the availability and accessibility of the necessary tools for a job. When the job is literacy, the relevance of all the above questions about the availability of clearly demarcated writing and book areas, as well as ample and varied supplies of paper and markers, becomes obvious. Accessibility is equally important for young literacy apprentices, so care must be taken with the placing of materials and tools so that they can be reached and replaced with ease by the children. The old adage of 'a place for everything and everything in its place' is important in any busy workshop and young children can be helped by informative labels on boxes, shelves, trays, cupboard doors and other surfaces. Labels should certainly include words – after all, literacy is the name of the game – but they can also feature drawings, photographs and template outlines of objects to facilitate replacing them.

Once this kind of practical workshop is set up young children begin to benefit from what I have clumsily called the philosophical/motivational characteristics of the setting. They are able to function as independent workers who know where to find the tools of literacy for themselves, but they can also share their knowledge with other children and involve adult practitioners in their investigations and learning. This control over the tools and the motives for literacy is immensely empowering for adults and for young children, and brings together the desire and the means for literacy. A literacy workshop is full of good reasons for reading and writing and rich in the tools with which to do so.

Workshops of any kind are places where people talk about the job in hand and also share stories about life, feelings and what novelists like to call 'the human condition' (figures 19 and 20). Literacy workshops in schools and other early years settings should be the same: children and adults need to talk about their lives and feelings, as well as about books, poems, stories, words, alphabets, names, letters, pens, paints, pictures – and everything under the sun! That is why an earlier chapter of this book outlined the links between language and thinking and why the checklist above has a section on speaking and listening. In a literacy workshop the links between thinking, speaking and literacy are close and self-evident.

The National Curriculum programmes of study for speaking and listening at Key Stages 1 and 2 (DFE, 1995) require a very broad range of opportunities for talk; from storytelling, play, drama and clarifying ideas to planning and predicting outcomes. There is no suggestion that this crucial foundation for literacy can be ignored, or that silent children doing copy-writing and completing worksheets will get ahead with the National Curriculum. There is also ample research evidence to suggest that the the workshop approach to literacy is just as relevant for older children (Harste, Woodward, Burke, 1984; Calkins, 1986; MacKenzie, 1992).

Only in a workshop setting can the range, variety, flexibility and full challenge of relevant literacy be ensured.

Sharing literacy

The notion of 'sharing literacy' should not be mistaken for some well-intentioned but unstructured approach in which adults randomly look at books with children and help them spell a few words. Very frequent sessions of shared reading and shared writing with both large (whole class) and smaller groups of children are central to good practice in the literacy workshop.

Figures 19 and 20   Classroom workshops: places where children and adults talk

Shared reading

This can be done with a few children and one teacher using a standard published book, but many children's books of high literary and artistic quality are now produced in a 'big book' format which enables a large group of children to see both print and illustrations comfortably. In regular shared reading sessions the teacher actively demonstrates and shares with the children all the skills and insights which an experienced reader brings to a text.

In practice this involves reading the text aloud to the children, firstly in one uninterrupted reading which establishes the plot of the story, the narrative style and the enjoyment of the illustrations. Second and third readings will begin to engage more closely with the text itself as the teacher points out the left to right flow of the printed words as they are spoken and highlights such interesting book conventions as title pages, authors' and illustrators' names and publishing details. Discussions of the plot, the characters and the tales being told by the illustrations develop the children's skills as discriminating and critical readers. Similarly, an ever closer focus on the print is also ensured by the teacher who draws the children's attention to recurring names, repeated phrases or rhymes, and words the children may know already from previous book readings, classroom word collections and labels, and the environmental print outside the school. Shared talk about all these meaningful words will most certainly be an appropriate teaching of phonics – phonics in action we might call it. Initial letter combinations like 'ch', 'th' and 'st', frequent end (terminal) groups and rhymes, common patterns in English such as 'qu', 'ou' and all the double vowel sounds occurring in such words as 'sleep', 'moo' and 'baa', enable children to identify and group words in 'families' and understand the code of written English. This close focus on print also enables teacher and children to talk about the nature and functions of punctuation as they encounter capital letters, full stops, commas, speech marks and the really exciting dashes, question marks and exclamation marks which occur in literature.

Shared writing

Shared writing is also a very specific teaching strategy. The conventions for writing English are taught through a partnership which involves children and teacher in writing together genuine and significant communications.

The necessary tools for this activity, which can be done with large and small groups of children, are a bold marker pen and a flip chart, or some large sheets of paper fixed to a small easel, or chalkboard. The topic for the writing is decided by group discussion and should arise easily from the many shared interests, activities and projects found in every classroom. It may on some occasions be appropriate to write a piece based on an individual's desire to share a personal experience. The length of the written message can be as short as a sentence of half-a-dozen words, or as long as the next 'chapter' of an ongoing group or class story; it will partly depend on the ages of the children and their past history as a writing group. What is important is the frequency of shared writing sessions and the quality of the literacy discussions which accompany them, not the word count!

The teacher-scribe writes to the dictation of the children, but talks herself and the children through every aspect of the process and draws the children's attention to the smallest details. In the first place this involves shaping up the group's discussion and fragments of speech into suitable contributions for writing down. At this first level the children are helped to make the important and complex move from speaking to writing: in a very real context the children learn that writing is different from speech. As they are helped to shape utterances into sentences they learn that writing does not rely on face-to-face contacts, gestures and voice intonations, but is self-sufficient, explicit and reliant on linguistic elements and conventions like punctuation to convey its meaning. The conventions of writing are taught as the teacher talks about, and also invites the children to instruct her in, all the fine detail of the decisions writers must make, for example:

- where do I start on the paper?

- do I use a capital letter?

- how do I spell that?

- what letter does it start with?

- do I know a word like it?

- have I used this word before?

- is this the end of this part?

- do I use a full stop here?

- how do I show that this is a question?

All these queries lead to constant rereading of the growing text, some rewritings of it, lots of linguistic talk and the energetic solving of genuine literacy problems (Geekie and Raban, 1993, p. 20).

Shared literacy approaches enable teachers and children to engage with the Range and Key Skills requirements of the National Curriculum for reading and writing. More importantly, they enable young children to behave as real readers and writers from the start (figures 21 and 22).

Figures 21 and 22   Real readers and writers at Key Stage 2 (eight- and nine-year-olds)

Making books

There is one other activity in the literacy workshop which helps children to learn all the processes and skills of reading and writing: the making of books. This has been mentioned briefly in the previous chapter, but the continuation and extension of this in the school years is crucial. As a literacy strategy it uses all the processes outlined in the discussion of shared literacy (above), but it enables individual children, or two or three in partnership, to become authors and illustrators and have work regularly 'published' for classroom and home use. At the heart of the strategy is a teacher (or other experienced adult) acting as a scribe and a child with a story to dictate. This partnership produces a text which can be refined in various ways for 'publication'; by the use of illustrations, photographs, typing, word-processing, traditional book-making techniques, or desk-top publishing. Achieving the finished product should not become a technical stumbling block; its value is as a significant writing experience and the creation of a text for reading. Its appearance should be as good as we can get it, reflecting respect for the beginner author's work, but it is not a professional publishing exercise. There are some practical guidelines for constructing books available for busy teachers and carers (Johnson, 1991).

A major study of the value of the approach draws attention to the triangular relationship between the composer/reader, the scribe/good listener, and the text which is written, read and edited (Smith, 1994). This author also gives detailed advice on writing books, reading books and training other adults, parents and older children as scribes and listeners.

We must not forget that in a classroom where materials and support for making books are always at hand, children will help each other to make books. In this way they increase their opportunities for being speakers, listeners, shapers of spoken into written language, writers, readers, editors, illustrators and book designers. These kinds of literacy partnerships also extend the children's grasp of the technical vocabulary of literacy and books, with appropriate talk about sentences, paragraphs, punctuation, double-spreads, end-papers and captions – the possibilities are immense!

Editing

One other great advantage of regular book-making in the literacy workshop is the impetus it gives to learning about editing and redrafting texts. This must be approached with some sensitivity in the early years of formal education, as any blanket demand for 'do it again in your best writing' to a young beginner writer who has spent much time and energy on her first written text could be counter-productive. The young writer who is beginning to write with confidence and producing considerable amounts of text is probably ready to discuss aspects of standardising some spellings and punctuation – some, but not everything at once. In the case of punctuation, the advice to children to read their texts aloud to a friend, or listen to someone else attempting to do so, is invaluable. After listening to the rhythms of their own writing spoken aloud, young authors can soon restore the meaning-carrying pauses and emphases to it by punctuating.

Using IT

For most children the first drafting, as well as any redrafting of text is made easier by the use of a word-processing program and the very youngest children can use picture and whole-word concept keyboards (Smith, 1994) to produce text which is satisfyingly legible and 'polished'. The use of IT is very motivating for children: it takes the strain of transcription out of the creative-composing process, it gives a professional-looking end product and it certainly makes children feel that they are writing for real with the technologies of their culture (figure 23). Teachers of literacy are also learning to value the literacy lessons which computers and word processors can provide: the need for spaces between words, alphabetic knowledge, varieties of scripts, upper and lower

Figure 23   Writing with the technologies of the future

case letter conventions, punctuation marks, page layout and so on. Word-processing programs can reinforce the main lesson of the literacy workshop: readers and writers must make constant decisions, solve problems and feel in control of their texts.

Handwriting

There has always been a strange inclination among many people to treat handwriting like cleanliness – next to godliness! It is still regarded as one of the touchstones of school success or failure, along with reading, and many parents believe that when a teacher is talking about 'writing' she is talking about handwriting. Many misunderstandings flow from this and we all need to be very clear about when we are referring to the process of writing and when to handwriting.

Writing is a main focus of this book. It is a cultural and creative intellectual process which enables us to use the conventional written symbols of a language in order to communicate our ideas, feelings and messages across time and space in a fairly permanent form.

Handwriting is a manual skill and a craft with artistic dimensions. It is concerned only with the formation of the written symbols used in a culture and as such it should be legible and pleasing. However, it becomes closely associated with cultural attitudes and the assumptions we make about individuals and can provoke strong feelings (Sassoon, 1995).

The early years workshop approach to literacy can provide good support for handwriting through appropriate provision, helpful examples of what it is and how to do it, and ample opportunities for practising it (figure 24). Teachers will need to set aside time to talk about handwriting and demonstrate the main strokes, not by plodding illogically through the alphabet, but by taking groups of letters which are formed by similar strokes. My own thinking on handwriting has been radicalised by the research and writings of Rosemary Sassoon and I would endorse her advice that tuition in the early stages must be individual and 'little and often' (Sassoon, 1993, p. 193). The excitement of Sassoon's approach lies in the emphasis on handwriting as the visible trace of a hand movement; the links with other motor and artistic activities (Davies, 1995); the support for finding comfortable and rapid personal styles; and the early introduction of 'exit strokes' on letters to facilitate the move towards joining up (cursive). There is little support from this expert for the rigid imposition of a whole school (or whole nation) script, or for imposed writing on lines for all young children at all times: flexibility of approach is the best guide.

Figure 24   Ample opportunities for practising handwriting; children at the start of Key Stage 2

Literature

Enriching and expanding children's experiences of literature must be a major priority for teachers of language and literacy. Early years classrooms can lay the foundations for literary understanding and create the prime motive for becoming literate. Young children need daily experiences of listening to literature, reading literature for themselves, and making and developing their responses to literature.

It is important that teachers, other professionals and families do not stop reading to children at the point when they are just beginning to be able to read for themselves. The human warmth and intimacy, the sheer pleasure and the good model of a skilled reader should not be withdrawn suddenly, leaving the 'just beginning' reader floundering slowly through print. Many less than confident young readers lose heart at this point and we should remember that the most sophisticated readers appreciate radio and audio-taped readings of stories, novels and poetry.

The teacher does need to vary and enrich the children's experiences of listening to stories by sometimes reading, over a period of days, longer books organised into chapters, or collections of tales about one central character.

Variety can be ensured by including readings of books with a factual element (*The Whales' Song*, Sheldon), or a historical dimension (*War Boy*, Foreman).

The classics

At the older end of the age phase there is much to be gained from introducing children to the acknowledged 'classics' of children's literature by reading such books as *Alice in Wonderland*, *Peter Pan and Wendy*, *Black Beauty*, *The Secret Garden* and *The Wind in the Willows*. I mention these specifically as they have been re-illustrated by distinguished modern artists who are equally famous for their own picture books; these and other classics do deserve a place in modern classrooms.

Myths and legends

Most early years teachers introduce children to a wide range of traditional folk and fairy tales and this material is also found in some of the popular reading schemes. We should not neglect, however, the rich variety of myths and legends (available in excellent modern editions) from such diverse cultures as ancient Greece, India, Scandinavia, the Celtic world, Africa and the Afro-Caribbean tradition.

Poetry

This book has already made much of the significance of poetry and rhyme in the early years: the early years classroom should be a wonderful place for playing with language and reading, collecting and talking about poetry. Many teachers find it helpful to create a particular focus on poetry and rhyme with a classroom poetry corner, table or shelf-unit which houses published collections of favourite poems, class-made anthologies, poetry and rhyme cards written (manually and electronically) and decorated by the children, and hoards of exciting words, riddles and tongue-twisters. Such a collection needs to be kept alive by enthusiastic poetry talk, the sharing of old favourites and new discoveries, as well as support and encouragement for children to write their own poetic language and experiment with poetic forms (figure 25).

Responding to literature

Response to literature is a complex matter at any level of education, but this does not excuse us from our responsibility for nurturing literary responses in the early years. At the very least we should give time and curriculum space to such important activities as talking about literature and many teachers are

the

Water drops

look like

colourless

and small Puddles,

and small balls.

By Natalie

Figure 25   Writing poetic language and experimenting with poetic form (six years four months)

beginning to experiment with ways of doing this (Robinson and King, 1995). Some of these approaches have been adapted from those used with older pupils, but in the early years we still need the faith and the patience to find children's literary responses surfacing in play, especially role-play and dressing up, in painting and drawing, or in modelling and constructing activities. Even the book-making approaches referred to above are a form of literary response when children take a famous formula and rework it, as in personalised versions of *Where's Spot?* or *Dr. Xargle*.

Children will certainly be able to express and explore their understandings of literature by being helped to re-enact the situations, characters and worlds of fiction, myth and history. Early years teachers might consider playing a more active part in drama work with children by using the 'teacher-in-role' technique familiar to most secondary English and drama teachers. Put simply, this means becoming a character in the drama and leading, supporting and stimulating the children's involvement – from the inside. A kindergarten research project in Sweden has achieved exciting results in raising the quality of play and literary awareness among children and adult practitioners by doing this (Lindqvist, 1995).

Book reviews

Written responses to literature have a place in the early years and children in the later early years can write reviews of books and poems, keep reading diaries or journals, contribute book recommendations to class newspapers and bulletin boards and produce brief book reviews for younger children in the school.

The teacher, Judith Crampton, who devised the form shown in figures 26, 27 and 28 explains:

> . . . *we found that children spent a lot of time retelling the story and we really wanted to draw out and develop their feelings, opinions, etc. Of course they could do this work in an exercise book but the format somehow seems to make it important for them and helps construct their work. They generally do one each week, though sometimes children may carry a book over two or even three weeks. Some children are planning their work at home and have sometimes brought in rough notes! They always have the books for reference of course, but on occasions children have been unhappy with their work and re-done it at home. These children are now seven and eight and have been doing these, once a week, for nearly a year. The folders of reviews comprise a good record of writing, reading, thinking development.*

Book Review

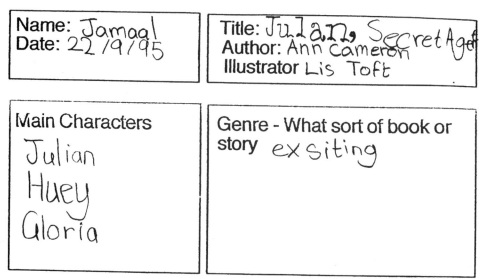

Name: Jamaal
Date: 22/9/95

Title: Julan, Secret Agent
Author: Ann Cameron
Illustrator Lis Toft

Main Characters

Julian
Huey
Gloria

Genre - What sort of book or story exsiting

Review - Write briefly what happens in the story

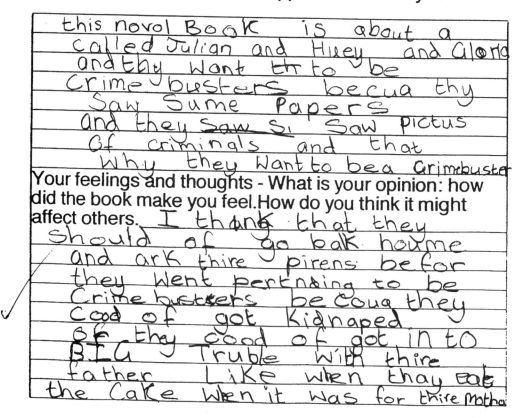

this novol Book is about a
called Julian and Huey and Gloria
and thy want thr to be
crime busters becua thy
saw sume papers
and they saw si saw pictus
of criminals and that
why they want to be a Crimebuster

Your feelings and thoughts - What is your opinion: how did the book make you feel. How do you think it might affect others. I thank that they
should of go bak howme
and ark thire pirens befor
they went perknsing to be
crime busters be coug they
cood of got kidnaped
or they cood of got in to
BIG truble with thire
father like when thay eat
the cake when it was for thire motha

Figure 26   Jamaal's review of Julian, Secret Agent *(seven years six months)*

Book Review

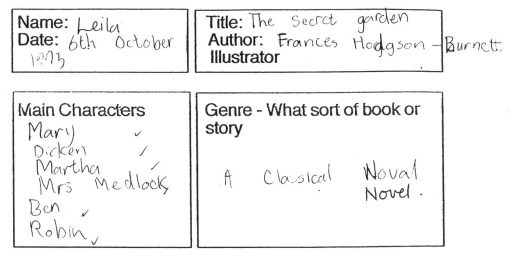

Name: Leila
Date: 6th October 1993

Title: The Secret garden
Author: Frances Hodgson-Burnett
Illustrator

Main Characters
Mary ✓
Dicken ✓
Martha ✓
Mrs Medlock
Ben ✓
Robin ✓

Genre - What sort of book or story

A Classical Noval Novel.

Review - Write briefly what happens in the story

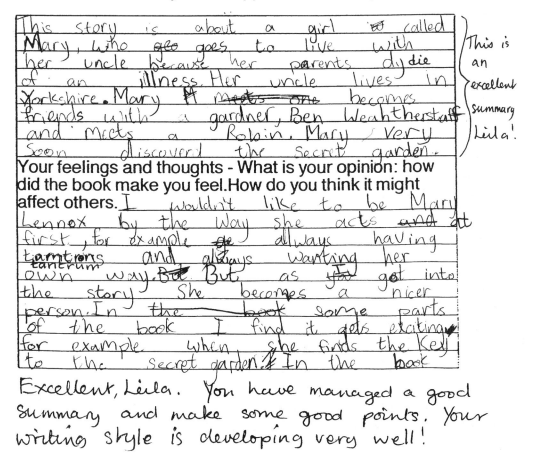

This story is about a girl called Mary, who goes to live with her uncle because her parents dy die of an illness. Her uncle lives in Yorkshire. Mary A meets one becomes friends with a gardner, Ben Weahtherstaff and meets a Robin. Mary very soon discovered the secret garden.

This is an excellent summary Leila!

Your feelings and thoughts - What is your opinion: how did the book make you feel. How do you think it might affect others. I wouldn't like to be Mary Lennox by the way she acts and at first, for example she allways having tamtrons tantrum and always wanting her own way. But But as I got into the story She becomes a nicer person. In the book some parts of the book I find it gets exciting for example when she finds the key to the secret garden. In the book

Excellent, Leila. You have managed a good summary and make some good points. Your writing style is developing very well!

Figures 27 and 28   Leila's two reviews of The Secret Garden

I would like to be Martha, as she is kind and thoughtful. When Martha was afraid of being sacked and was almost crying I felt horrible. She was a really nice person and I can't bear the thought of someone like her being scared scared like that. I also like Robin and Dicken. Dicken can charm animals and know all about plants. Dicken is in Martha's brother. This book is in some parts old English and has some Yorkshire in it. This book I think is suitable for 82 eight year olds and older. Mary has Mary has a cousin named Colin who lived also with her uncle. Colin was her uncle's son. His mother had died when he was born. He was a very ill person. Mrs Med Medlock, the house keeper tries to keep him a secret from Mary But mary soon discovered him.

Book Review

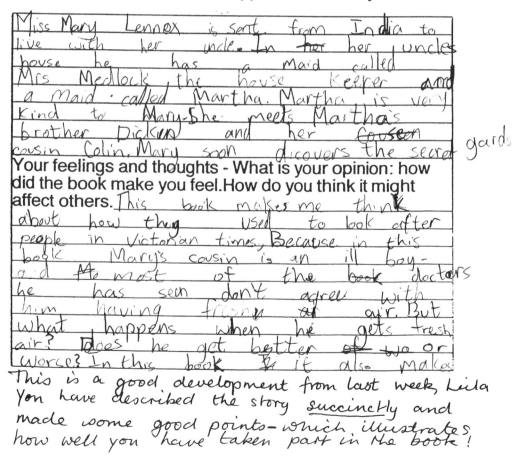

Name: Leila **Date:** 13th October.	**Title:** The Secret Garden **Author:** Frances Hodgson-Burnett **Illustrator**

Main Characters Mary Lennex ✓ Colin. ✓ Dicken ✓ Martha ✓ Mrs Medlock. ✓	**Genre - What sort of book or story** A Classical Novel ✓

Review - Write briefly what happens in the story

Miss Mary Lennex is sent from India to live with her uncle. In her uncles house he has a maid called Mrs Medlock the house keeper and a maid called Martha. Martha is very kind to Mary. She meets Martha's brother Dicken and her cousin Colin. Mary soon discovers the secret garde

Your feelings and thoughts - What is your opinion: how did the book make you feel. How do you think it might affect others. This book makes me think about how they used to look after people in Victorian times. Because in this book Mary's cousin is an ill boy- and the most of the book doctors he has seen don't agree with him having fresh air. But what happens when he gets fresh air? Does he get better or worse? In this book it also makes

This is a good development from last week, Leila. You have described the story succinctly and made some good points- which illustrates how well you have taken part in the book!

Figure 28

Me think about people who have tantrums lots of the time, because in the begining Mary is a bit like that. But also when Mary met colin she thought that colin was always having tantrums and was also having a tantrum. I think this book would be suitable for eight and older. I would like to be Dicken if I were to chose a boy. If I were to chose a girl I wouldnt mind being a Mary Lennox. Dicken is an animal charmer and Mary is the main charecter.

Excellent!

BEING A LITERACY TEACHER

Being a literacy teacher is a demanding and complex role and all of the discussions in this book are relevant to it. The purpose of this section is to focus on some core activities, starting with the nature of the literacy teacher's role.

The role: expert and extender

The teacher of literacy is, or must become, an expert in two areas – linguistics and literacy. The early years teacher of initial literacy must also be an expert in child development and young children's learning – a true pedagogue whose expertise is explored in all the books in this series.

The first two chapters of this volume detailed the kinds of linguistic understanding which the early years educator requires. When teaching early literacy we must be aware of the nature and variety of language, the significance of talk and narrative and the differences between spoken and written language, as well as the range of different literacies inside and outside the school setting.

The teacher's expertise in literacy is built on to this linguistic foundation and involves knowledge of the early stages of symbolic representation, mark-making and experimental writing (Chapter 4). Other aspects of literacy expertise include the teaching of reading and writing; the study of written language systems including the conventions of spelling, syntax and punctuation; and being an expert observer and assessor of children's literacy skills and understandings. These aspects will be discussed below.

The notion of the literacy teacher as an extender of children's literacies is central to the role and an important counter-argument to the misguided belief, found among the non-experts, that teachers no longer teach literacy. Detailed accounts of teaching methods for shared reading, writing and the making of books were given above and other ways of extending children's literacy in the early years of schooling follow.

The reading teacher

It often seems that the reading teacher is a victim of controversy, trapped between the distorted public debates about methods and materials, the political need for scapegoats and the high expectations of families. The issue of families will be addressed in the following chapter and the political dimension of literacy goes far beyond the focus of this book. However, more informed public debates about literacy, allied with an ability and willingness on the part of teachers to talk about their approaches to teaching children to read (Whitehead, 1992), would make it less easy for politicians to blame all the ills of society on reading teachers while ignoring the close links between poverty and low literacy levels (Maclure and French, 1981; Lake, 1991).

Sensible talk about teaching reading is still side-tracked by two so-called debates which are caricatures of the real issues. I am, of course, referring to 'phonics versus look-and-say' and 'real books versus reading schemes'. The first of these 'debates' is a crude simplification about reading methods and still persists, although few, if any, professional and experienced teachers of reading are going to rely solely on either when teaching children to read English. Both methods have a place in a battery of useful strategies, but more is required. The National Curriculum Orders for Reading at Key Stage 1 (1995) reflect the recent upsurge of interest in phonological awareness and phonic knowledge, but they also retain some emphasis on such important strategies as enjoyment of literature, a wide exposure to books of many kinds, word recognition, and contextual and grammatical understanding. Effective reading teachers have to ignore the dafter extremes of controversy and make it possible for beginners to draw on and use a wide range of strategies, the major ones being:

- semantic (using meaning, pictures and context) *'Why is the baby crying?'*

- syntactic (linguistic and grammatical) *'Does that make sense?'*

- grapho-phonemic (phonological awareness and knowledge) *'What sound does it start with? Do you know that letter?'*

- bibliographic (books and literary conventions) *'Where do we start to read? Where is the title?'*

The debate about what reading materials to use in the initial teaching of literacy is caricatured as a battle between diehard adherents of reading schemes and equally fanatical real books people. The reality is more sober and more complex, although in literary terms I would expect all teachers of literacy to be passionate lovers of books and tireless campaigners for sharing books with children of all ages. The ill-informed 'books or schemes' debate also tends to mask the fact that children read all kinds of materials in the course of the school day in a lively early years setting. Indeed, they need many opportunities for reading and looking through books every day, sometimes alone and silently (figure 29), sometimes reading with other children and adults (figure 30). The goal of learning to read should be so that you can do it for yourself, with a huge variety of materials and for a wide range of purposes.

Figure 29   Silent reading for pleasure in school

Figure 30   Enjoying reading with friends in school

Reading must not be thought of as that strange public performance when a child reads aloud to an adult and gets a page number recorded somewhere, or even a 'new book'. Reading aloud to a teacher is a specific teaching and diagnostic assessment exercise and on a few occasions it will be for the purposes of making a summative assessment of a child's progress. This cannot be hurried and is best done regularly, rather than daily, with an emphasis on the quality and depth of the session. It is a priority and other time-consuming activities may well have to take second place to high-quality reading teaching.

Many teachers use an initial reading scheme as one way of presenting children with ready-organised and controlled texts which are an indicator of some levels of successful reading. The dangers in too heavy a reliance on such materials are:

- they present children with a limited experience of what reading could be about;

- they are frequently third-rate in terms of the quality of the language, story and illustrations;

- they mislead parents and some teachers into thinking that the scheme itself teaches reading.

The reverse of this particular argument applies when critics claim that using real books is a way of failing to teach reading. In fact, the regular use of books of real literary quality requires the same teaching skills as were outlined in the discussion of shared reading, plus the keeping of detailed records:

> *Notes must be kept on the learner's range of strategies for tackling unknown words and print, and the apparent degree of understanding of narratives (pictorial and linguistic), of irony, under-statement or omissions, and the nature of the child's affective responses to, and comprehension of, the many issues raised by literary and factual texts. The nature of mistakes or misreadings must be analysed carefully, not just corrected . . .*
> (Whitehead, 1992, p. 7)

This is not an easy option and it is a lot more demanding on the teacher than working with the over-simplified text of a reading scheme book. Conversely, the over-simple scheme text can be more difficult for the child because of its distance from normal spoken and written language patterns, its often meaningless repetition and very thin plot. Real books do have support from SCAA and the DFE: the Key Stage 1 tasks for reading assessment (1995) suggest for Level 1, and require for Level 2, books of undoubted merit and great popularity with young children.

Despite conscientious teaching and good classroom provision for literacy, there have always been children and adults who struggle with reading or fail to make any progress. While not being in any way complacent, we should not be surprised that so complex a psychological, linguistic and cultural process causes difficulty for a number of children. However, parents, carers and early years teachers should not allow themselves to be stampeded into accepting increasingly earlier interventions, quick-fix cures and dubious medical excuses for children's difficulties with literacy. It is often the case that these children require far longer exposure to all the provisions for language and literacy discussed in this book and far greater intensity of adult support. Some recent innovations designed to recover lost ground with children who are slow to get started on reading (and writing) do offer intensive one-to-one support and a wide range of literacy activities. The dangerous interventions, which have failed children for generations, are those which remove young children from all the rich play and language and literacy activities of the early years setting and give them drills and meaningless exercises. In other words, giving them even less reading and writing than other 'successful' children.

Another danger for children in the UK is the fact that we start our young children in formal schooling so early, sooner than any other comparable country in the developed world, and therefore put early and enormous pressure on them to study literacy in a formal way. This is another reason for teachers of initial reading to resist the early identification and labelling of very young children as 'failing readers'. These kinds of labels do their own sad work and children and their families are diminished by them; it is far better to give children and literacy a chance in the early years and expect reading to be a life-long learning process.

Extending reading

The reading teacher has a responsibility to extend children's experiences of reading and this must certainly be a feature of the early years classroom. One aspect of this will be the widening range of literature to read and to listen to, discussed above, but children also need to read more than fiction and narrative.

Most children have some problems with adjusting to non-fiction and information texts because, although they may be written in a chronological narrative, they use a style which is very different from spoken and literary genres. This non-fiction style has long, complex sentences; uses passive verb forms and has the detached, tentative voice we associate with scientific writing and information books.

Considerable research has been done in recent years on children's reading of non-fiction and non-narrative texts (Mallett, 1992; Neate, 1992) and although this work has a direct reference to work in the later primary years it has some implications for early years education. Young children will need specific help in reading and understanding non-fiction and non-narrative texts. They will need to have ample opportunities for discussing the issues and questions they want to bring to information texts, and because they will need to consult these kinds of texts for their own purposes and in order to get on with meaningful activities, children should make an early start on using:

- cookery books;

- word and picture dictionaries;

- identification books on birds, flowers, shells, insects and so on;

- street maps, atlases, bird's-eye-view plans, aerial photographs;

- patterns and instructions for making puppets, models and so on.

Children will need to discuss with each other and with adults what sense they are making of their encounters with non-fiction and information texts.

Making their own information and instruction texts will help young children explore the linguistic style and the organising principles of the genre. It is also another area in which alphabetic knowledge and study skills can be reinforced as the children plan and produce contents lists, indexes, diagrams, maps and step-by-step instructions.

The reading teacher will need to bring a wide range of non-fiction materials into the classroom, including such everyday examples as telephone directories, local guides, advertising copy, knitting patterns, newspapers, weather and sports reports, timetables and television guides (also a great help with the conventions of recording the time). All this material is cheap or free, and provides a host of insights into the many different kinds of reading we do in a literate society of great complexity.

Extending writing

As with reading, the early years literacy teacher must extend children's experiences of writing in a variety of genres, not just narrative. The earlier sections of this chapter recommended making writing materials available in all the classroom areas so that appropriate writing is done for science investigations, shopping lists, invitations and play in pretend hospitals, hairdressers and homes.

Extending this basic approach can include the study of the many different types of letters we are likely to receive and this has been made joyfully easy by *The Jolly Postman* books (Janet and Allan Ahlberg). With the aid of this delightful series, children can analyse and giggle over the genres of mail order correspondence, solicitors' letters and seaside postcards and then create their own versions of such letters for the postman's or postwoman's sack.

The classroom news and bulletin board suggested earlier can lead to the study of the styles used in print journalism and public notices and might result in setting up a class newspaper office in order to publish a class paper. Visits to a local newspaper office, or visits to the class by journalists, will increase the children's interest in writing, particularly as they realise that 'writing' can be a profession or hobby. Local poets, novelists and children's writers are an inspiration in schools and can raise the status of writing in a school and its community dramatically. The hidden bonus in all this visiting, in and out of school, is that it demands even more special kinds of writing as invitations are sent and thank you notes composed.

One other area of specialist writing which can be easily developed and extended in the early years classroom is the creation of scripts for drama work, puppet plays and the inhabitants of the miniature worlds found in the sand, water, blocks, space stations and dolls' houses of most settings. Script writing is usually cooperative writing, even in the professional worlds of radio and television, and requires children to work together and pool their literacy strengths and their creative ideas. It is also a kind of writing which is constantly redrafted and very open-ended, a contrast to the formal certainties of solicitors' letters and public notices.

Finally, it must be remembered that all the suggestions for extending reading given earlier are themselves ways of extending writing, as children produce their own local guides, instruction booklets for caring for class pets, and dictionaries.

Teaching about spelling

Many of the discussions in this and the previous chapter have touched on spelling and indicated the ways in which the early years setting can increase children's understanding of the conventions for representing sounds and words in English. In all their reading and writing young children are encountering the standardised spelling of written English and this is an immensely significant support. In addition to all of this, the role of the teacher in the school years, and definitely not just the early school years, is to do two things:

- to collect, analyse and correct the children's own misunderstandings about spelling patterns;

- to give the children self-help strategies for spelling.

The first task involves teachers and other adults in keeping good records and conscientiously reading children's written work, in order to collect frequently mis-spelled words which can be discussed with individual writers as well as with small groups, or even a whole class. Certain patterns regularly confuse children and adults, and can be usefully talked about and investigated closely by all the children in a group or class – sometimes! It is important to pick up the non-standard spellings which occur in children's own writing because these are reflections of their current interests and 'getting them right' will matter to the children. It is even more important to teach about spelling in an inspiring and reassuring way if we want children to love language and writing. Our aim should be to make non-standard spelling an interesting event and a stimulus for research and cooperation, not a crime punishable by humiliation.

This takes us to the issue of self-help strategies which go well beyond the 'learn these by Friday for a test' school of spelling. It is possible to draw on all the complex visual and motor processes involved in writing certain patterns of letter groups, in very simple ways, in order to help children learn spellings. The system was originally formulated by Peters (1985) and highlights the importance of visual feedback in spelling. It can be simplified into a basic guide for the young writer:

LOOK closely at the word you wish to learn

COVER it up

WRITE the word as you remember it

CHECK your attempt against the original word

REPEAT this pattern, if you had an error, until you can write the word.

This technique can be used by anyone at any age and is a positive way of turning 'bad spellers' into independent learners who are engaged in the study of their written language – or languages.

Language study

This daunting sounding topic now appears, twinned with Standard English, in the National Curriculum Orders for English at all Key Stages (1995). However, the study of language has been a central part of language and literacy teaching in early years classrooms for a long while – we just call it by different names. For example, all of the suggestions in this chapter and the preceding one are aspects of language study and cover the National Curriculum requirements that children should play word games, talk about the language used for special occasions and in special genres like traditional stories, discuss word meanings, extend their vocabularies, differentiate between spoken and written forms and recognise standard English varieties. Perhaps all that can be added to this are some comments on broadening and enjoying language study with young children.

Many educators with a linguistic background now refer to the importance of *metalinguistics* or *metalingual awareness* in the teaching of language and literacy and this is yet another daunting title for an important aspect of language study. It refers to the specialist words we use for talking about language in its spoken and written forms, and has implications for the 'words about words' which we enable children to investigate and use themselves.

Children need to understand what we mean when we refer to 'words', 'letters', 'sounds', 'capitals', and even 'sentences'; they particularly need to know that this is a special language and may be different from their common-sense, or cultural use of the same terms. Some children think that 'numbers' (numerals) are letters and many wonder about the link between a mark on a page (another technical term) and the 'letter' which comes through the letter-box. And what about the 'sound' from the upstairs TV and the little meaningless noise the teacher is asking you to make? Even older children need to sort out 'capitals' from media references to London or Delhi, and they may have associations with 'sentences' other than the meaning which linguists struggle to clarify. We need to remember that some of these terms are complex and controversial in the world of linguistics, so we cannot give children simple definitions to learn. These terms are only to be understood in use and that is the secret of success for children – they need to be talking, reading, writing and sorting out and refining the labels as they need them and use them.

Word meanings are best developed and discussed in the pleasurable context of reading and listening to literature. The poetic and the playful use of language should be familiar to children from nursery rhymes, songs and nonsense and take them from speculations about 'runcible spoons' and 'ladles' to the language of *The Iron Man* (Hughes) and the play with syntax and colour terms in *Mr. Rabbit and the Lovely Present* (Zolotow and Sendak).

Literature can also be a great stimulator of classroom investigations into language variety and language change. Literature is doubly powerful in that it constantly exposes children to written standard English and can also extend their experience of varieties of English and the changes in English over time. Some of the classics referred to earlier reflect change in written standard English and children will notice the different rhythms and choices of words in *A Little Princess* and *The Secret Garden*, for example. In the latter case they will also become aware that an attempt has been made to represent the Yorkshire dialect forms used by servants and the poor. This is, perhaps, a first lesson in the social discrimination associated with spoken non-standard English. The use of dialect words can also be studied in *The Mousehole Cat* (Barber and Bayley) and I know of two young children who went so far as to make a star-gazy pie with their mum and can chant the list of Cornish fish names as if it were a magic spell:

> *ling and launces, scad and fairmaids, morgy-broth.*

Another kind of English is skilfully represented in the tale of *Flossie and the Fox* (McKissak) where, within the folktale convention of the resourceful small child who outwits a predatory fox, we read the cadences, words and sentence structures of black American English from the deep south. This is cleverly set against the narrator's standard written American English and the arrogant fox's country gentry way of speaking.

Other areas of the curriculum which support the study of language change and variety are drama, writing for different purposes, puppetry, and talk about advertising and the media. The children themselves, their families and communities are also rich resources for language study and early years educators can think about classroom surveys of the languages and dialects the children speak and are beginning to write, from odd words to full fluency. Teachers and other adults in the school can contribute to these opportunities to celebrate with pride the linguistic richness of a class, school or other setting. These surveys can be undertaken outside the setting to include families and the community. Literacy surveys of what uses are made of reading and writing in the children's homes, communities and wider society can begin modestly with children questioning their parents, carers and shopkeepers; collecting written information from buses, post offices and stations; and looking at street names and road signs.

Records and assessments

It is now widely understood that children's errors in reading and writing are a source of valuable insights for the teacher: they are windows on the mind and on the mental processes involved in acquiring and using literacy (Goodman, 1982). This means that teachers' ongoing records of children's literacy need to be rich in detailed observations and subject to careful study and analysis. Something of this significance has been recognised and retained in the Key Stage 1 English Tasks for reading and writing and the Handbook for 1995 offers some general guidance on how to talk to young children about their knowledge of literature and books. This guidance also covers the making of a running record of a child's reading of a passage from a real book. The use of descriptive levels for making summative assessments of children's achievements in speaking and listening, reading and writing is to be welcomed in that it places professional judgements about children's attainments back in the hands of their teachers. There is nothing spuriously accurate and numerical about the descriptive sentences we have been given to work with and it would be wise for early years professionals to seize this opportunity to develop procedures for pooling and moderating together their records and judgements, prior to assigning levels to children's work.

It is possible to detect in the current tasks fragments of the good practices in monitoring and assessing children's language and learning pioneered in the Primary Language Record (CLPE/ILEA, 1988). This approach is still used by many teachers because:

- it goes well beyond summative assessments;

- it provides ample diagnostic insights for the teacher;

- it reflects the richness and breadth of children's language experiences and potential;

- it involves parents and primary carers directly in contributing to their children's cumulative language records.

In order to build up sufficiently rich records of children's language and literacy, notes and observations must be collected on responses and developments in the relevant curriculum areas: talking, listening, stories, books, poetry, rhyme, music, dance, print, signs, drawing and pictures.

Reading profiles should include notes on children's approach to texts, their knowledge about illustrations, print and the clues offered by context, syntax, phonics and semantics. When children read aloud the teacher must note any attempts to self-correct, their questions about the text and any other evidence of making sense of the task. Examples of individual children's errors need to be recorded on a copy of the text and teachers can use or adapt their own symbols for recording and analysing miscues (Money, 1987; Barrs and Thomas, 1991).

Monitoring children's progress as writers is best done by collecting samples of mark-making, drawing and writing at regular intervals. These can be simply labelled to record name, date, age and context in which the work was produced. The teacher's own record should be a brief analysis of what the child knows about print: is there evidence of messages, signs, conventional and invented letter forms, numerals, linearity, directionality, spelling conventions, digraphs ('ch', 'sh'), letter strings ('. . . ing'), double letters ('ss', 'oo'), punctuation, style and genre (letters, advertisements, instructions)?

Finally, the children themselves should be involved on a regular basis in talking about their own views of their progress as readers and writers. These comments can be dictated to an adult, or written by children who can do so, and included in both diagnostic and summative assessments. Children should certainly choose some of the written material to be kept in their folders for the record system and this work should be accompanied by their own brief reasons for their choices.

Detailed discussions of assessment and record-keeping in early childhood can be found in *Assessment in Early Childhood Education* (Blenkin and Kelly, 1992) and *Getting to Know You* (Bartholomew and Bruce, 1993).

6 TALKING WITH PARENTS AND CARERS ABOUT LANGUAGE DEVELOPMENT

All through this book there are references to children developing language and learning about literacy with parents, carers and families in a variety of local communities, home languages, cultures and traditions. This final chapter will pull together these central issues in child language development and make some suggestions for working together in children's best interests. However, this is not primarily a book about parental involvement in education and for a full background to the topic I would recommend an earlier volume in this series which is focused on Pen Green Centre for the under-fives and their families: *Learning to be Strong* (Whalley, 1994). Practitioners who are concerned mainly with the early years of statutory schooling will find equally powerful evidence and insights in *Parents and their Children's Schools* (Hughes *et al.*, 1994).

The focus in this chapter will be on the nature of the partnership with parents and carers; the role parents and carers play in early literacy; and ways of talking about language development for parents, carers and practitioners.

PARTNERSHIP WITH PARENTS AND CARERS

Worthwhile talk about children's language development depends on a sound approach to practitioner and parent partnerships, so it is crucial that we examine our ideas about partnership.

Partners

Partners are equals, although they often have different roles and different kinds of expertise, and partners can be as unalike as any other individuals. When the partners are parents or carers and the practitioners who work with their children in a range of early years settings, there is lots of scope for misunderstanding these different roles and lots of scope for improving mutual respect and insight. We all need to understand the distinctive roles we play as parents and practitioners.

Parents

Parents are as different as the rest of humanity and cannot be lumped together as 'the parents' – indeed, many of them are early years practitioners and professionals! They bring many cultures, traditions, languages, temperaments, histories, strengths and weaknesses to their parenting roles.

Parents are more knowledgeable about their own children than anyone else can ever be: they have a deeper emotional commitment to them and a wider background of experiences shared with them than can ever be achieved in institutions which have the children for a comparatively few hours. Even when parent–child relationships are apparently poor and ineffective, they are still a potent factor, to be respected and handled with great sensitivity.

Parents care about what happens to their children, now and in the future, and they are particularly concerned about what happens to them in early years care and education settings.

Practitioners

Practitioners who work with children are expert in relating to large numbers of children; they can observe them closely, manage and organise them in groups, and they develop warm professional relationships with them as individuals.

Practitioners have considerable knowledge, both practical and theoretical, about children's normal development and deviations from these norms. They understand how to engage children's interests, how to structure learning and how to provide worthwhile activities for them. The best practitioners know when to intervene and when to stand back in children's learning and investigations.

Practitioners are as individually different as parents – many of them are parents – and can be limited by their own histories, backgrounds and languages.

Practitioners may have more access to, and understanding of, government legislation and the many official agencies which affect the care, education and lives of young children and their families.

What are the implications for partnerships between such different and interesting people?

Clearly such diversity can only be handled successfully and in children's best interests if the partnership is open, democratic and based on consultation and respect. We have to know what our partners are doing and what their aims and aspirations are for the children who have brought us together. This means that creating effective channels of communication and sharing information will be crucial (Hurst, 1991). It is easy to give examples of the ways in which many early years settings do this, but the danger is that this can become very one-sided, with the flow of information and arrangements always coming from the professional side. Of course it is good to have family rooms on the premises, family noticeboards and newsletters, open sessions and workshops, talks and outings, and even a prominent description of the curriculum followed and the current focus for play and learning. But there must also be a more open kind of permanent invitation to parents and carers to say what they want, ask for particular activities, identify what puts them off coming to the setting, or what they find to be pointless, or even offensive. I have in mind here the occasional objection to finger painting, or a deeply felt disapproval of children being allowed to play naked in very hot weather. Good partners respect such feelings, talk about them, and explore possible compromises. This is particularly important for families who are new to a setting. Furthermore, they have a right to be fully consulted about their level of involvement in the gradual settling in of their children and about any home visits prior to their children's first attendance at the setting. Partnerships depend on mutual respect, trust, some shared goals and the acceptance of differences. These are not achieved instantly – we all have to work at being good partners.

Consumers

Once young children move into schools in the state-maintained sector their parents and carers find that they have a set of new rights which are intended to make them 'consumers' rather than partners. This change has been brought about by the 1988 Education Reform Act (DES) and the Parent's Charter (DES, 1991) and reflects a government decision to turn education into something like a free market where schools will compete for the custom of parents and parents will pick and choose and sample what is on offer. This market is now being expanded to include non-statutory provision of all kinds for the under-fives by the introduction of government 'nursery vouchers' and this raises a few questions. What is available? What is being consumed? Who are the consumers? Where are the children in all of this? These are questions to be debated long and passionately, but some simple answers are interesting.

- Available goods: these consist solely of the National Curriculum and its compulsory assessment procedures, or desirable outcomes in non-compulsory settings.

- The consumables: it is not possible to hand out learning, or knowledge, to be swallowed like a vitamin pill or a burger.

- The consumers: the only genuine 'consumers' are the children themselves in the schools and early years settings.

- The children appear to be the passive recipients of whatever is chosen for them and done to them.

This is an unacceptable picture of young children's care and education, from the perspectives of parents, carers, practitioners and the children themselves. A recent research project focused on Key Stage 1 has reached the same conclusions (Hughes *et al.*, 1994) and highlights the facts that parents have had no real voice in these changes; do not wish to be consumers; choose schools on the grounds of size and friendliness; appreciate their local schools and teachers; find the National Curriculum basic and lacking in fun and are critical of the disruption to their children's education caused by SATs (Standardised Assessment Tasks).

However, many of the parents in the research described above did not feel that they had enough information about what their children were learning in school, despite plentiful contacts. This suggests that we must continue to work at true partnerships, real conversations and cooperation.

Co-workers

In most early years settings, including statutory schools, parents can be found working alongside professional practitioners. This makes for unique opportunities in partnership approaches to early years care and education, because there is nothing like hands-on involvement with groups of children, alongside a colleague, to make sense of routines and curriculum activities. In these kinds of situations it is much easier for co-workers to ask each other questions, challenge assumptions, demonstrate how to do something, share their expertise and experience, or talk about ideas and anxieties.

When we are working for children as a mixed group of parents, practitioners and even multi-professionals, we learn an important lesson about education: it is social and collaborative. This is just as true for adult learning as it is for young children's learning. Every solitary scholar has a back-up team of tutors, librarians, family, friends and fellow scholars waiting to talk it all through, disagree and offer comfort. Similarly, every child in the sandpit wants someone to eat their 'pie', identify the ingredients and discuss the best method for cooking it.

As co-workers we may have the beginnings of an answer to the problem of finding enough practitioners of high quality to work with young children. We can create networks of learning and self-improvement. We can, for example, undertake shared action research into our own practice and seek to raise the quality of our work with young children (Blenkin and Paffard, 1994). There are many historical precedents for this kind of self-help; perhaps we should not desire to recreate ragged schools and hedge schools, but we could take a pride in becoming together paint-smeared and clay-daubed scholars and partners!

Parents, carers and early literacy

First educators

It is obvious that the great majority of parents are their children's first carers, but we now find a broad agreement that parents are also their children's first and most enduring educators. This consensus has been reached partly because of Piaget's pioneering studies of infant thinking in the earliest weeks and months of life, a period when it is parents, or other primary carers, who create the child's environment and the resulting stimulus for the rapid development of the brain. Linked to this evidence for the continuity of human learning from birth are the powerful modern studies of babies' sociability, and their ability to share feelings and states of mind in partnership with their parents and carers (Trevarthan, 1993). The third and final piece of evidence for learning with parents and carers is the everyday but stunning achievements of almost every baby: learning to communicate, talk, use narratives and become aware of marks and print. These achievements have been discussed in detail in this book and the point to be made here is that the role of parents in early learning, particularly language learning, is the foundation of all later educational success.

Many parents, across all social and economic classes, are very active in their role as first educators of their young children. Research has demonstrated that they talk in stimulating and challenging ways to their children; share books, songs, stories and jokes with them; teach them to play card games, make cakes, count and identify letters; and keep them supplied with markers and scrap paper (Wells, 1981; Tizard and Hughes, 1984; Tizard et al., 1988). This evidence that parents teach their children has not always been welcomed and developed in early years settings. However, when professional practitioners have invited families to take an active part in monitoring and supporting their children's cognitive developments the outcomes for children, parents and practitioners have been very positive (Athey, 1990; Nutbrown, 1994). In no area has this been more fully developed than in early literacy, as the following examples indicate.

Babies and books

Perhaps there have always been 'bookish' families who share books with their babies (White, 1954; Butler, 1979), but in recent years there have been some determined efforts to help many more parents do this (figure 31). One of the

Figure 31   Reading for pleasure at fifteen months

most well-planned and carefully evaluated was the *Bookstart* pilot project in Birmingham which involved the city's library services and the South Birmingham Health Authority. *Bookstart* packs containing a book, a poetry card, a poster, an invitation to join the local library and other information were given free to 300 parents/carers of nine-month-old babies in three areas of the city by the local health visitors. The project covered a wide ethnic and social-economic cross-section of the city and the families were asked to complete questionnaires at the start of the project and six months later. The evidence from the parents was that sharing books with baby spilled over into an enthusiastic sharing of books with all the family, including toddlers, older children and adults. In some families it also sparked off, or renewed, an interest in joining the public library and even buying books. The *Bookstart* scheme has now been extended to Sunderland, West Sussex and Hertfordshire and librarians and families report the same enthusiasm for sharing books, buying books and joining libraries. The evaluators of the Birmingham pilot study draw our attention to its significance by pointing out that it is about more than early reading and school achievement, or even combating adult illiteracy and crime:

Books are sources of shared and repeated pleasure, of insight and new knowledge and of new possibilities for living.
(Wade and Moore, 1993a)

Charting early literacy

Increased knowledge about the emergence of literacy (Hall, 1987) in the earliest years of childhood has aroused a great deal of interest in the part played in the process by families, communities and cultural beliefs and activities. One powerful example of involving families on a full partnership basis is the Sheffield Early Literacy Development Project (Weinberger, Hannon and Nutbrown, 1990).

The approach of the researchers was based on asking families to share with them the ways in which they already helped their young children to get into literacy. Not surprisingly the parents talked about looking at labels on tins and signs in shops, writing notes together, looking at books and eating alphabet spaghetti (Nutbrown, 1994, p. 89)! In return the researchers helped the parents to link their existing good practices to the broad patterns of language development and provided them with a literacy progress chart. This was designed as a sheet of interlocking jigsaw shapes, each of which named an achievement which could be coloured in by a parent or carer once it was noted. The chart covered looking at environmental print, beginning to write and sharing books; it provided a record of progress, from making marks to writing own name, or from telling stories about the pictures in a book to recognising the name on a food wrapper.

This research noted that parents supported early literacy in three ways: they were 'models', that is, they did it themselves; they provided opportunities for literacy for their children; and they recognised their children's efforts as readers and writers (Nutbrown, 1994).

Reading at home

The previous examples have been focused on babies and children under five, but perhaps the largest number of projects about parents and literacy are concerned with reading in the early stages of primary school. There are many ways of doing this (Topping and Wolfendale, 1985; Bloom, 1987), but some consistent attempts to ask parents to hear children read at home and share books with their children are made by most infant/primary schools. The sight of young children taking their 'book-bags' home each afternoon is now a part of the national scene, as is the classroom morning session of 'changing' books and handing teacher a parental comment card on the home reading progress. These important partnerships in reading have a common ancestor in the research done in Haringey in the 1970s which indicated that reading at home with parents was more effective in improving children's reading progress than any other kind of school support (Hewison and Tizard, 1980). Research continues to indicate that pre-school literacy experiences and long-term parental interest and involvement in children's reading at home, combined with genuine consultation between teachers and parents/carers about school-based help such as Reading Recovery (Wade and Moore, 1993b), make all the difference to progress in reading.

TALKING ABOUT LANGUAGE DEVELOPMENT

Finding the right form of language in which practitioners, parents and professionals can talk together about children's language development is a continuing challenge. It has been one of the main difficulties of writing this book and the problem it has set remains. How do we use straightforward language and yet do justice to the complexity of individual language development in the years before eight? There does not appear to be an easy answer, but we have to keep on talking . . .

OUR CHILDREN'S LANGUAGE

About communicating, talking and listening

We are all conversational partners for our children. We are all models for our children of how to use language. The daily caring, talking, playing and routine reading and writing we do with our children shapes their language development and their thinking.

Our babies communicate with us long before they talk – they do it from birth. They get in touch by gazing at us, making faces at us and by moving their hands, arms, legs and toes in response to our attention and our voices. We become skilled at listening to our babies and watching them closely. This helps us to get to know them and interpret their messages and their meanings; it helps us to share our lives and activities with them. Our babies become talkers by communicating without words and by constantly watching and listening to all that goes on around them.

We tend to share our conversations and little stories about the ups and downs of daily life with wakeful and attentive babies and toddlers. We even expect responses from them. So we look at them, pause in our talk and give them time to find the appropriate sounds or words. Later, we tell them the words they ask for or seem to need, and we repeat important words or phrases frequently. We really make it possible for them to give names to their world and talk about it.

Our children begin by talking about the people they know, the events of their days, their own feelings, the food they eat, their toys, animals and family pets, and their own feelings and ideas about things. These topics of conversation remain very important all our lives and our children learn to talk about them by telling stories. Their conversations with us are full of little tales about falling down, losing things, meeting people, seeing animals or cars, feeling frightened or finding something interesting. These are everyday stories of 'what happened and how I feel about it'; they are not very different from the stories in family reminiscences, TV 'soaps', novels and myths.

There are many people who worry that television and video have changed all this talking between children and carers. On the positive side, we know that television is an important part of all our lives and our children grow up with it. They learn an enormous amount about the wider world beyond their homes and they hear a wide range of languages, voices, accents and plenty of standard English on it. However, it is still a one-way kind of communication in most homes and we should think about trying to watch as much as possible with our babies and young children. We can talk to them about what they have watched and even try to follow up some programmes by drawing and making things, dressing up, going on visits, finding books, singing songs, repeating rhymes and poems, doing some cooking or dancing round the room!

Television can be an excellent child 'minder' and entertainer, although too much sitting and watching is not healthy in terms of children's physical development and their need for frequent exercise. But any potential threat to very young children's language development is only likely to materialise if watching TV totally takes the place of playing, helping and talking between young children and caring adults – and older children.

About writing and reading

It is not an exaggeration to say that learning to become a writer and a reader depends on already being a talker and listener (or a signer if deaf), and a gossip and storyteller. It also depends on finding out what is involved in writing and reading.

So, once again it is clear that children's first literacy teachers are their parents and families, followed by their surroundings and communities. We demonstrate writing for our children every time we scribble a shopping list, sign a document or fill in a form. We demonstrate reading for them every time we open a letter, read the instructions on a food package or flick through a newspaper. And these are only the most basic examples of daily literacy. Surroundings and communities swamp all of us with examples of what print looks like and how it works. Everywhere we take our children we can find exciting free reading materials to point out, talk about and play with: from leaflets and carrier bags to road names and advertising posters. And we should not forget to talk about 'reading' the meanings of signs like traffic lights, the symbols on traffic signs, and familiar logos in supermarkets and fast food restaurants.

But our babies and toddlers do not just wait to be taught, so let us think about them, in a sense, as their own best teachers. They show us what they have noticed and what they are interested in every day and they can teach us a thing or two about becoming literate in any language.

What are the signs that our very young children are starting to write and read the languages of our homes and communities?
They will show some interest in print and notice it everywhere: including letters, numbers, the writing on clothes labels, in shops and on buses. They may point to print and ask about it.

They will try to make print-like marks when they are drawing and painting, or using raw pastry or plasticine, or writing with their fingers on steamed up windows and in spilt drinks or food!

They may ask us for help and advice, saying, 'read that letter to me', 'what does that say?', 'can I write something?'

They will almost certainly want endless supplies of paper scraps, notepads, felt pens, biros, pencils, paints, chalks and crayons. And they will love plastic and magnetic letters, or rubber letter and date stamps and ink pads. With these materials they will be keen to write 'pretend' lists, letters, cards, labels, invitations and little books.

They will really enjoy owning and borrowing picture books, story books, information books, and even mail order catalogues. They will often show great affection for the books, or the pictures and characters in them, sometimes stroking the pages lovingly. These favourites are frequently hidden in special places or taken everywhere – to the potty or lavatory, to bed, or into the child's own preferred hidey-hole like a cupboard or under a table. Of course our children will ask us, or other special people, to read these precious books to them and we might have to struggle if it is a seed catalogue or a car handbook!

Our young children will be fascinated by listening to people and will tune in immediately to stories, jokes, gossip, poems, common sayings, songs and rhymes. They will also ask for some of these to be repeated again and again. They will insist on listening to favourite stories and books repeatedly and soon know them 'off by heart' and begin to join in with repetitive or amusing bits. They may also talk about favourite characters and their adventures, and some children will act out, dress up as, or draw and 'write' these stories.

They will certainly play and have fun with languages, especially with rhymes, nonsense, songs, tongue-twisters, brand names, advertising slogans and any rude words they come across. They will love dancing and twirling around at any time or place, as well as singing, stamping and clapping rhythmically, and taking part in traditional games, pastimes and rituals such as parties, carnivals, festivals and religious ceremonies.

They will begin to recognise and name some letters, particularly the initial letters of their own name, or letters in the names of family, friends, favourite sweets, drinks and food, or popular TV programmes. This will mean that they know quite a number of letter names and some of their usual 'sounds', so it is a good idea to start looking at really attractive alphabet books, as well as making home-made ones for fun. This can be started by cutting letters from magazines and leaflets and sticking them in scrap books, or on scrap paper.

They will begin to write their name, or special mark, on their books, drawings and other property and cover sheets of paper or the margins of newspapers and the covers of magazines with what almost looks like writing. There will probably be identifiable letters, or numbers, or even the child's name among these important scribbles. At this point, many children ask adults and older children to write names and brief stories down for them and clearly enjoy this chance to dictate to a helpful secretary.

What difference will compulsory school make?

In one sense it should not make much difference, because all that has gone on and just been described here is the very best kind of language and literacy development (figure 32). Teachers should be planning to continue and build on all the good things that have gone on in homes, care centres, playgroups and nursery settings. They will also be extending what we as parents, carers and early years professionals have begun with our children.

Teachers should still be setting up classrooms with ample opportunities and materials for talking, drawing, reading and writing. They will aim to show children all the many uses of literacy and find enjoyable ways of presenting them with the need to read and write every day. One of their top priorities will be to inspire children with a love of stories, poetry and books: they may tell us that they want our children to be 'hooked on books'!

Figure 32   'The best kind of language and literacy' – using story props for Goldilocks and the Three Bears *in a Croydon nursery school*

Teachers will be good listeners, tireless secretaries and enthusiastic publishers. They will always be willing to write for our children, listen to them read and tell stories, and make attractive books with them. This is where they may ask for our help as occasional classroom listeners, readers and secretaries to the children. One enthusiastic teacher with more than 30 children can almost work miracles, but parents working alongside teachers can definitely transform children's lives.

Teachers will introduce our children to computers and word-processing programs, not just for speed and smart copy, but as one way of teaching them more about how the written forms of language work. Teachers will emphasise the spelling, grammar and punctuation of written standard English, but only as our children become more confident and enthusiastic as writers. However, children who do not use English in their homes and communities should be supported and helped in their first language in school, if at all possible, while they develop some level of bilingualism. Talking, reading and writing in their home languages is central to children's thinking and self-respect and should be encouraged in every way possible. Furthermore, this actually helps with the development of fluency and literacy in English.

Most teachers are unlikely to believe that there is only one way to teach reading that will work for every child. This is because reading is a very complicated mix of thinking skills and experiences. Consequently, teachers of reading generally prefer carefully planned mixing and matching of methods. They do introduce children to the sounds of letters and groups of letters like 'th', 'ch' and 'ing', but only as children's confidence with reading and sharing books increases. Plenty of experience with books is essential because children need to recognise instantly many English words which just cannot be sounded out. Just imagine trying to sound out 'said', 'thought' or 'night'! As a reader of words like this you are also helped enormously by the sentence or situation in which you meet the word. This is a warning to all of us to let children read interesting material and not just meaningless lists of words. The most important help for our children comes from having a good idea of what a whole book or story is about, what the pictures are suggesting, and what is likely to happen.

It is now absolutely clear that if parents and carers share books with their children at home, including those books they bring from school, they make a huge contribution to their success at reading. When teachers hear children read at school they have a different responsibility. They keep careful notes about how our children use clues such as the whole context of the book, the pictures, the meaning and sense of words, their knowledge of sounds and ability to sound out unknown words, and their ability to go back and correct themselves. This is how teachers assess children's reading development and decide what help and what kind of reading our children need next. Reading from a 'reading scheme' book is only one way of assessing reading and these books do not actually 'teach' reading. Children have to learn about print and books for themselves and many will find the process slow and boring if they only meet scheme books.

The best cure for some problems in the early years of reading is to return to all the approaches used before compulsory schooling, in order to rebuild a child's confidence and enjoyment of books and print. Go on sharing books and writing together as much as possible; struggling, uninterested readers need more books, more stories and lots more being read to. Most of all they need to know that someone who loves them believes in them totally and knows that one day they will be a reader.

We cannot separate language development from the rest of our lives and teach it separately to our children. What they do successfully with language, they do as part and parcel of doing really important things. Things like telling us about their quarrels, celebrating their good times, reading their names on labels, or writing a message of kisses on a letter to a far-away grandparent. Throughout our lives language development is bound up with just being ourselves.

Bibliography

Aitchison, J. (1994) *Words in the Mind. An Introduction to the Mental Lexicon*. Oxford: Blackwell.

Arnberg, L. (1987) *Raising Children Bilingually: The Pre-School Years*. Clevedon: Multilingual Matters.

Athey, C. (1990) *Extending Thought in Young Children. A Parent-Teacher Partnership*. London: Paul Chapman.

Baker, C. (1993; 1996) *Foundations of Bilingual Education and Bilingualism*. Clevedon: Multilingual Matters.

Barrs, M. and Thomas, A. (eds.) (1991) *The Reading Book*. London: CLPE.

Bartholomew, L. and Bruce, T. (1993) *Getting to Know You. A guide to record-keeping in early childhood education and care*. London: Hodder and Stoughton.

Beard, R. (1987) *Developing Reading 3–13*. London: Hodder and Stoughton.

Beard, R. (ed.) (1995) *Rhyme, Reading and Writing*. London: Hodder and Stoughton.

Bennett, M. (ed.) (1993) *The Child as Psychologist. An introduction to the development of social cognition*. Hemel Hempstead: Harvester Wheatsheaf.

Bissex, G. L. (1980) *GNYS AT WRK: A Child Learns to Write and Read*. Cambridge, Mass.: Harvard University Press.

Blenkin, G. M. and Kelly, A. V. (eds.) (1992) *Assessment in Early Childhood Education*. London: Paul Chapman.

Blenkin, G. M. and Paffard, F. (1994) 'Telling Verona's Story – A Search for Principles in Practice'. In *Early Years*, Autumn, 15, 1, pp. 30–36.

Bloom, W. (1987) *Partnership with Parents in Reading*. Sevenoaks: Hodder and Stoughton/UKRA.

Britton, J. (1992) *Language and Learning. The importance of speech in children's development*. Harmondsworth: Penguin.

Bruce, T. (1987) *Early Childhood Education*. Sevenoaks: Hodder and Stoughton.

Bruner, J. S. and Haste, H. (eds.) (1987) *Making Sense. The Child's Construction of the World*. London: Methuen.

Bryant, P. E. and Bradley, L. (1985) *Children's Reading Problems*. Oxford: Blackwell.

Butler, D. (1979) *Cushla and her Books*. Sevenoaks: Hodder and Stoughton.

Butler, D. (1995) (3rd. edit.) *Babies Need Books*. Harmondsworth: Penguin.

Calkins, L. M. (1986) *The Art of Teaching Writing*. Portsmouth, NH: Heinemann.

Campbell, R. (1995) *Reading in the Early Years Handbook*. Buckingham: Open University.

Carnegie Corporation of New York (1994) *Starting Points. Meeting the Needs of Our Youngest Children*. New York: Carnegie Corporation.

Centre for Language in Primary Education/Inner London Education Authority (1988) *The Primary Language Record. Handbook for Teachers*. London: CLPE.

Chomsky, N. (1957) *Syntactic Structures*. The Hague: Mouton.

Chukovsky, K. (1963) *From Two to Five*. Berkeley: University of California Press.

Clark, E. V. (1982) 'The Young Word Maker: a case study of innovation in the child's lexicon'. In *Language Acquisition: The State of the Art*, E. Wanner and L. R. Gleitman (eds.). Cambridge University Press, pp. 390–425.

Clark, M. M. (1976) *Young Fluent Readers*. London: Heinemann.

Cochran-Smith, M. (1984) *The Making of a Reader*. Norwood, NJ: Ablex.

Copperman, C., Kanter, H., Keiner, J. and Swirsky, R. (eds.) (1989) *Generations of Memories. Voices of Jewish Women*. London: The Women's Press.

Crystal, D. (1987; 1997) *The Cambridge Encyclopedia of Language*. Cambridge University Press.

Davies, M. (1995) *Helping Children to Learn through a Movement Perspective*. London: Hodder and Stoughton.

DES, Department of Education and Science (1975) *A Language for Life. (The Bullock Report)*. London: HMSO.

DES, Department of Education and Science (1988) *The Education Reform Act. The School Curriculum and Assessment*. London: HMSO

DES, Department of Education and Science (1991) *The Parent's Charter*. London: DES

DFE, Department for Education (1995) *English in the National Curriculum.* London: HMSO.

DFEE, Department for Education and Employment (1995) *Quality Assurance Regime for Institutions which redeem Pre-School Education Vouchers: Discussion Paper.* London: DFEE.

DFEE, Department for Education and Employment (1996) *Nursery Education Scheme. The Next Steps.* London: DFEE.

EYCG, Early Years Curriculum Group (1992) *First Things First, Educating Young Children. A Guide for Parents and Governors.* Oldham: Madeleine Lindley.

EYCG, Early Years Curriculum Group (1995) *Four-Year-Olds in School: Myths and Realities, Action Paper 2.* Oldham: Madeleine Lindley.

Engel, D. M. and Whitehead, M. R. (1993) 'More First Words: A Comparative Study of Bilingual Siblings'. In *Early Years*, Autumn, 14, 1, pp. 27–35.

Ferreiro, E. and Teberosky, A. (1982) *Literacy before Schooling.* London: Heinemann.

Freire, P. and Macedo, D. (1987) *Literacy. Reading the Word and the World.* London: Routledge and Kegan Paul.

Gardner, H. (1991) *The Unschooled Mind. How children think and how schools should teach.* London: Fontana.

Geekie, P. and Raban, B. (1993) *Learning to Read and Write Through Classroom Talk.* Warwick Papers on Education Policy No. 2. Stoke-on-Trent: Trentham.

Goodman, K. S. (1982) 'Miscues: Windows on the Reading Process'. In *Language and Literacy: The selected writings of Kenneth S. Goodman* (Vol. 1), F. K. Gollasch (ed.). London: Routledge and Kegan Paul.

Goswami, U. and Bryant, P. E. (1990) *Phonological Skills and Learning to Read.* Hove: Lawrence Erlbaum.

Gregory, E. and Kelly, C. (1992) 'Bilingualism and Assessment'. In *Assessment in Early Childhood Education*, G. M. Blenkin and A. V. Kelly (eds.). London: Paul Chapman, pp. 144–162.

Gregory, R. L. (1977) 'Psychology: towards a science of fiction'. In *The Cool Web*, M. Meek, A. Warlow and G. Barton (eds.). London: Bodley Head, pp. 393–398.

Hall, N. (1987) *The Emergence of Literacy.* Sevenoaks: Hodder and Stoughton.

Halliday, M. A. K. (1975) *Learning How to Mean. Explorations in the Development of Language*. London: Arnold.

Hamers, J. F. and Blanc, M. H. A. (1989) *Bilinguality and Bilingualism*. Cambridge University Press.

Hardy, B. (1977) 'Towards a poetics of fiction: an approach through narrative'. In *The Cool Web*, M. Meek, A. Warlow and G. Barton (eds.). London: Bodley Head, pp. 12–23.

Harris, M. (1992) *Language Experience and Early Language Development: From Input to Uptake*. Hove: Lawrence Erlbaum.

Harste, J. C., Woodward, V. A. and Burke, C. L. (1984) *Language Stories and Literacy Lessons*. Portsmouth, NH: Heinemann.

Heath, S. B. (1983) *Ways with Words. Language, Life and Work in Communities and Classrooms*. Cambridge University Press.

Hewison, J. and Tizard, J. (1980) 'Parental involvement and reading attainment'. In *British Journal of Educational Psychology*, 50, pp. 209–215.

Holdaway, D. (1979) *The Foundations of Literacy*. London: Ashton Scholastic.

Houlton, D. (1986) *Cultural Diversity in the Primary School*. London: Batsford.

Hughes, M., Wikeley, F. and Nash, T. (1994) *Parents and their Children's Schools*. Oxford: Blackwell.

Hughes, T. (1995) 'Myth and Education'. In *Celebrating Children's Literature in Education*, G. Fox (ed.). London: Hodder and Stoughton, pp. 3–18.

Hurst, V. (1991) *Planning for Early Learning. Education in the First Five Years*. London: Paul Chapman.

Johnson, P. (1991) *A Book of One's Own*. London: Hodder and Stoughton.

Jones, D. and Medlicott, M. (1989) *By Word of Mouth. The Revival of Storytelling*. London: Channel 4 Television.

Lake, M. (1991) 'Surveying all the factors. Reading research'. In *Language and Learning*, 6, pp. 8–13.

Lally, M. (1991) *The Nursery Teacher in Action*. London: Paul Chapman.

Lindqvist, G. (1995) *The Aesthetics of Play. A Didactic Study of Play and Culture in Preschools*. Uppsala, Sweden: Uppsala University.

MacKenzie, T. (ed.) (1992) *Readers' Workshops. Bridging Literature and Literacy.* London: Paul Chapman (for Irwin Publishing, Toronto).

Maclure, M. and French, P. (1981) 'A comparison of talk at home and at school'. In *Learning Through Interaction. The Study of Language Development*, G. Wells (ed.). Cambridge University Press, pp. 205–239.

Mallett, M. (1992) *Making Facts Matter. Reading Non-Fiction 5–11*. London: Paul Chapman.

Martin, T. (1989) *The Strugglers*. Milton Keynes: Open University.

Matthews, J. (1994a) *Helping Children to Draw and Paint in Early Childhood. Children and Visual Representation*. London: Hodder and Stoughton.

Matthews, J. (1994b) 'Deep Structures in Children's Art: Development and Culture'. In *Visual Arts Research*, Fall, 20, 2, pp. 29–50.

Mills, R. W. and Mills, J. (1993) *Bilingualism in the Primary School. A Handbook for Teachers*. London: Routledge.

Money, T. (1987) 'Early Literacy'. In *Early Childhood Education. A Developmental Curriculum*, G. M. Blenkin and A. V. Kelly (eds.). London: Paul Chapman, pp. 139–161.

NCC, National Curriculum Council/National Oracy Project (NOP) (1990) *Teaching, Talking and Learning in Key Stage One*. York: NCC.

Neate, B. (1992) *Finding Out about Finding Out. A Practical Guide to Children's Information Books*. London: Hodder and Stoughton/UKRA.

Nelson, K. (1973) 'Structure and Strategy in Learning to Talk'. In *Monographs of the Society for Research in Child Development*, 38 (1–2, serial no. 149).

Nelson, K. (1989) *Narratives from the Crib*. Cambridge, Mass.: Harvard University Press.

Newkirk, T. (1984) 'Archimedes' dream'. In *Language Arts*, 61, 4, pp. 341–350.

Nutbrown, C. (1994) *Threads of Thinking. Young Children Learning and the Role of Early Education*. London: Paul Chapman.

Paley, V. G. (1981) *Wally's Stories. Conversations in the Kindergarten*. Cambridge, Mass.: Harvard University Press.

Paley, V. G. (1986) *Mollie is Three. Growing Up in School*. Chicago: University of Chicago.

Payton, S. (1984) 'Developing awareness of print. A young child's first steps towards literacy'. In *Education Review Offset Publication No. 2*. University of Birmingham.

Pennac, D. (1994) *Reads Like a Novel*. London: Quartet Books (1992, Paris: Gallimard).

Peters, M. L. (1985) *Spelling Caught or Taught? A New Look*. London: Routledge and Kegan Paul.

Raban, B. (1988) *The Spoken Vocabulary of Five-Year-Old Children*. Reading: University of Reading, Reading and Language Information Centre.

Redfern, A. (1993) *Practical Ways to Teach Spelling*. Reading: University of Reading, Reading and Language Information Centre.

Redfern, A. and Edwards, V. (1992) *How Schools Teach Reading*. Reading: University of Reading, Reading and Language Information Centre.

Roberts, R. (1995) *Self-Esteem and Successful Early Learning*. London: Hodder and Stoughton

Robinson, M. and King, C. (1995) 'Creating communities of readers'. In *English in Education*, Summer, 29, 2, pp. 46–54.

Sacks, O. (1989) *Seeing Voices. A Journey into the World of the Deaf*. Berkeley: University of California Press (1990, London: Pan Books).

Sassoon, R. (1990) *Handwriting: a new perspective*. Cheltenham: Stanley Thornes.

Sassoon, R. (1990) *Handwriting: the way to teach it*. Cheltenham: Stanley Thornes.

Sassoon, R. (1993) 'Handwriting'. In *Teaching Literacy: Balancing Perspectives*, R. Beard (ed.). London: Hodder and Stoughton, pp. 187–201.

Sassoon, R. (1995) *The Acquisition of a Second Writing System*. Oxford: Intellect.

Saunders, G. (1988) *Bilingual Children: From Birth to Teens*. Clevedon: Multilingual Matters.

SCAA, School Curriculum and Assessment Authority (1996) *Nursery Education Consultation. Desirable Outcomes for Children's Learning on Entering Compulsory Education*. London: SCAA.

Schaffer, H. R. (ed.) (1977) *Mother-Infant Interaction*. London: Academic Press.

Scrivens, G. (1995) ' "Where's the 'K' in Emergent Literacy?": Nursery Children as Readers and Writers'. *In Early Years*, Autumn, 16, 1, pp. 14–19.

Selinker, L. (1992) *Rediscovering Interlanguage*. London: Longman.

Sheridan, D. (1979) ' "Flopsy, Mopsy and Tooth": the storytelling of preschoolers'. In *Language Arts*, 56, 1, pp. 10–15.

Smith, B. (1994) *Through Writing to Reading. Classroom strategies for supporting literacy*. London: Routledge.

Smith, B. H. (1980, 1981) 'Narrative versions, narrative theories'. In *On Narrative*, W. J. T. Mitchell (ed.). Chicago: University of Chicago Press, pp. 209–232.

Smith, F. (1988) *Joining the Literacy Club*. London: Heinemann.

Spencer, M. M. and Dombey, H. (1994) *First Steps Together. Home-School Early Literacy in European Contexts*. Stoke-on-Trent: Trentham.

Stern, D. (1977) *The First Relationship: Infant and Mother*. London: Fontana.

Styles, M., Bearne, E. and Watson, V. (eds.) (1992) *After Alice*. London: Cassell.

Tizard, B., Blatchford, P., Burke, J., Farquhar, C. and Plewis, I. (1988) *Young Children at School in the Inner City*. Hove: Lawrence Erlbaum.

Tizard, B. and Hughes, M. (1984) *Young Children Learning. Talking and Thinking at Home and at School*. London: Fontana.

Topping, K. and Wolfendale, S. (eds.) (1985) *Parental Involvement in Children's Reading*. London: Croom Helm.

Trevarthen, C. (1993) 'Playing into Reality: Conversations with the Infant Communicator'. In *Winnicott Studies*, Spring, 7, pp. 67–84.

Vygotsky, L. S. (1986) *Thought and Language*. Cambridge, Mass.: MIT Press (revised and edited by A. Kozulin).

Wade, B. and Moore, M. (1993a) *Bookstart in Birmingham. A description and evaluation of an exploratory British project to encourage sharing books with babies*. Book Trust Report 2. London: Book Trust.

Wade, B. and Moore, M. (1993b) 'Reading Recovery: Parents' Views'. In *English in Education*, Summer, 27, 2, pp. 11–17.

Weinberger, J., Hannon, P. and Nutbrown, C. (1990) *Ways of Working with Parents to Promote Literacy Development*. Sheffield: University of Sheffield, Division of Education.

Weir, R. H. (1962) *Language in the Crib*. The Hague: Mouton.

Wells, G. (ed.) (1981) *Learning Through Interaction*. Cambridge University Press.

Whalley, M. (1994) *Learning to be Strong. Setting up a neighbourhood service for under-fives and their families*. London: Hodder and Stoughton.

White, D. (1954) *Books Before Five*. New Zealand: Council for Educational Research.

Whitehead, M. R. (1985) 'On Learning to Write. Recent research and developmental writing'. In *Curriculum*, 6, 2, pp. 12–19.

Whitehead, M. R. (1986) ' "Breakthrough" Revisited. Some thoughts on "Breakthrough to Literacy" and developmental writing'. In *Curriculum*, 7, 1, pp. 26–32.

Whitehead, M. R. (1990a) *Language and Literacy in the Early Years*. London: Paul Chapman.

Whitehead, M. R. (1990b) 'First Words. The Language Diary of a Bilingual Child's Early Speech'. In *Early Years*, Spring, 10, 2, pp. 53–57.

Whitehead, M. R. (1992) 'Failures, Cranks and Fads: Revisiting the Reading Debate'. In *English in Education*, Spring, 26, 1, pp. 3–14.

Whitehead, M. R. (1994) 'Stories from a Research Project: Towards a Narrative Analysis of Data'. In *Early Years*, Autumn, 15, 1, pp. 23–29.

Whitehead, M. R. (1995) 'Nonsense, Rhyme and Word Play in Young Children'. In *Rhyme, Reading and Writing*, R. Beard (ed.). London: Hodder and Stoughton.

Young, P. and Tyre, C. (1983) *Dyslexia or Illiteracy?* Milton Keynes: Open University.

Literature referred to in the text
(excluding books listed in Chapter 3)

Ahlberg, Janet and Allan, *Bye Bye Baby*. London: Heinemann.

Barrie, J. M. *Peter Pan and Wendy* (illus. Michael Foreman). London: Pavilion Books.

Burnett, Frances Hodgson, *The Secret Garden* (illus. Shirley Hughes). London: Gollancz.

Burningham, John, *Oi! Get Off Our Train*. London: Jonathan Cape.

Burningham, John, *The Shopping Basket*. London: Jonathan Cape.

Carroll, Lewis, *Alice's Adventures in Wonderland* (illus. Anthony Browne). London: Walker Books.

Dunbar, Joyce and Varley, Susan, *Lollopy*. London: Andersen Press.

Foreman, Michael, *War Boy*. London: Pavilion Books.

Furchgott, T. and Dawson, L., *Phoebe and the Hot Water Bottles*. London: Andre Deutsch.

Grahame, Kenneth, *The Wind in the Willows* (illus. Justin Todd). London: Gollancz.

Hill, Eric, *Where's Spot?* London: Heinemann.

Keller, Holly, *Geraldine's Blanket*. London: Julia MacRae.

Kent, Jack, *The Fat Cat*. London: Hamish Hamilton.

Nicoll, Helen and Pienkowski, Jan, *Meg and Mog*. London: Heinemann.

Rosen, Michael and Oxenbury, Helen, *We're Going On A Bear Hunt*. London: Walker Books.

Sewell, Anna, *Black Beauty* (illus. Charles Keeping). London: Gollancz.

Sheldon, Dyan and Blythe, Gary, *The Whales' Song*. London: Hutchinson.

Waddell, Martin and Firth, Barbara, *Can't You Sleep Little Bear?* London: Walker Books.

Zolotow, Charlotte and Sendak, Maurice, *Mr Rabbit and the Lovely Present*. London: Bodley Head.

INDEX